The Border l _____gു

*The story of the witchcraft trials
of the Scottish Borders*

1600 – 1700

Mary W. Craig

To Lynn

May

Published in 2008 by
Border Voices Community Interest Company,
Galashiels Road, Stow,
Scottish Borders, TD1 2RA

Woodcuts images courtesy of the Museum of Witchcraft,
Boscastle, Cornwall

ISBN 978-0-9560774-0-0

---

*Mary W. Craig is originally from Glasgow but now lives and works in the
Borders village of Stow. A researcher by profession, Mary's other published
works include a contribution to Scotlands of the Future and several works
of poetry published in the Poetry Now anthologies. She has also written the
story of Madeleine Smith, the Victorian socialite found not proven of murder.
A member of her village parish archive group and keen local history enthusiast,
Mary's hobbies include walking in the Border hills and reading.*

Printed and Bound by Meigle Colour Printers Ltd.,
Galashiels, Scottish Borders

Acknowledgements

This book was written in an attempt to cast light on the social history surrounding the witch trials that took place in the Scottish Borders in the 17th century. The book is not, and would not claim to be, an authoritative text book on the phenomenon of witch trials in the Borders but is an attempt to tell some of the stories of the ordinary women and men of the Borders who were caught up in the trials.

I am indebted to the many professional historians who have previously written on the subject of witchcraft in Scotland. Their meticulous research provided much of the background understanding on witchcraft for this book.

The records held at the National Archives of Scotland have proved invaluable in compiling this book as has the University of Edinburgh's Survey of Scottish Witchcraft. I also wish to thank the Museum of Witchcraft in Boscastle, Cornwall for the use of several woodcut images and general background information. They hold a large and very fascinating library and collection on witchcraft for those interested in the subject.

I am grateful to my colleague, Graeme McIver, for reading this manuscript and offering invaluable help, advice and corrections, any residual errors remain entirely my own.

Mary W. Craig

List of Illustrations

1. 17th century woodcut of four men in front of an enthroned goat-headed Devil.

2. 17th century English woodcut of trio of malefice witches.

3. 1582 woodcut of four witches. One climbing a tree, one stirring a cauldron, one holding a stang or pitchfork and one riding a goat.

4. 1555 woodcut showing two witches, female with an upturned cauldron and the male with an animal skull on a staff, raising a storm. A ship is sinking in the background.

5. 16th century woodcut showing ithyphallic Horned God, with goat's ears, horns and legs, holding broom and candle, surrounded by a circle of tiny dancing figures.

6. 17th century woodcut showing lady of quality flying on a goat.

7. 1643 woodcut of the witch of Newbury, in puritan dress, standing on a floating plank.

8. 1489 woodcut of witches holding a cockerel and a snake over a cauldron raising bad weather to destroy crops.

9. 16th century woodcut showing three witches hanging on the gallows, a witch holding her ferret familiar, and toads and other familiars in the foreground.

Cover woodcut: 16th century German woodcut of the Devil riding off with a witch.

Inside cover: The Stow Parish Record of 1649.

Contents

'It being known that many persons of both sexes, unmindful of their own salvation and straying from the Catholic Faith, have abandoned themselves to devils, incubi and succubi, and by their incantations, spells, conjurations, and other accursed charms and crafts, enormities and horrid offences, have slain infants yet in the mother's womb, as also the offspring of cattle, have blasted the produce of the earth, the grapes of the vine, the fruits of the trees, nay, men and women, beasts of burden, herd-beasts, as well as animals of other kinds, vineyards, orchards, meadows, pasture-land, corn, wheat, and all other cereals; these wretches furthermore afflict and torment men and women, beasts of burden, herd-beasts, as well as animals of other kinds, with terrible and piteous pains and sore diseases, both internal and external; they hinder men from performing the sexual act and women from conceiving, whence husbands cannot know their wives nor wives receive their husbands; over and above this, they blasphemously renounce that Faith which is theirs by the Sacrament of Baptism, and at the instigation of the Enemy of Mankind they do not shrink from committing and perpetrating the foulest abominations and filthiest excesses to the deadly peril of their own souls, whereby they outrage the Divine Majesty and are a cause of scandal and danger to very many.'

Papal Bull of Pope Innocent VIII, 1484

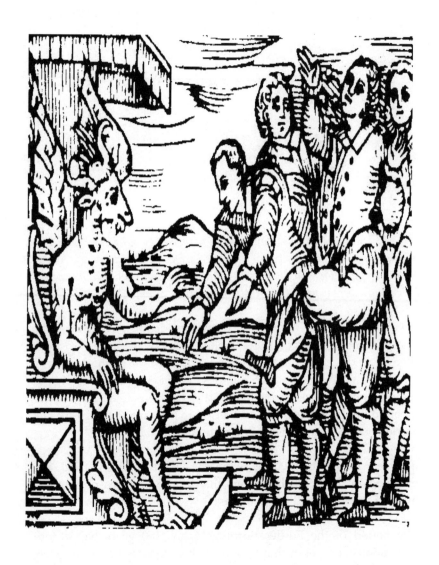

1. INTRODUCTION

'a century of death'

he century started with plague and ended with famine. Between those two, death and torture would be visited upon three hundred and fifty two individuals across the Borders. The crowns of Scotland and England would be united, a king would lose his head and men would go to war over the correct form of worship. And in the villages and towns of the Borders local men and women would watch as neighbours were worriet (throttled) and burnt.

It was to be a century of suspicion, torture and death. It would claim the lives of some and ruin the lives of many more. By the time it was over there was scarcely a village or town in the Borders that had not been affected. There were few communities that had not seen a neighbour dragged off to face interrogation, torture and possible death. It was a period of unremitting fear and terror orchestrated by the Kirk and carried out by a complaisant and compliant civil authority.

Between 1600 and 1700 more witches were accused, tried and executed in the Scottish Borders than any other area of Scotland except Edinburgh and the Lothians.

The period of the Border Burnings spans 100 years barely four generations and yet in that time over three hundred and fifty were dragged off to gaol to be ill treated, tortured and interrogated. Trials were conducted in all four of the Border counties: Berwickshire,

1

Peeblesshire, Selkirkshire and Roxburghshire. And in towns and villages alike pyres were built, tar barrels were filled and victims burnt. The total numbers of those who died may never be fully known but piecing together what records exist a conservative estimate for the Borders is that around two hundred and eighteen women and men faced the rope and flames.[1]

While the reasons for the Scottish witchhunts have been extensively documented elsewhere, *Maxwell-Stuart et al*, little, if any, attention has been paid to the particular nature of the witch hunts in the Border lands. Why, with a relatively small and sparse population, did the Borders manifest such a large crop of witches and why did the local Presbytery pursued them with such evident vigour?

For such a rural and sparsely populated part of the country, the Borders showed a particular intensity in its zealous prosecution of witches. The hunt for witches in the Scottish Borders appears to have been characterised by levels of religious zeal seldom seen elsewhere. This was not the simple relief at having consigned one of the Devil's own to the flames, or the peace of mind that an evil doer had been removed from a community. The Borders Kirk truly believed that they were attacked by the Devil because of their Godliness. The greater the number of witches, the more pious must be the Kirk and so, perversely, the Kirk became drawn into denouncing more and more witches. Religious fervour quickly became hysteria as the line between spiritual ecstasy and delusional frenzy was crossed.

To put the Scottish witchhunts into some perspective, the rate of trials and executions in Scotland per head of population was around ten times higher than the comparable rate in England. To put the Borders witchhunts into perspective, the rate of trials and executions was the second highest in Scotland and was ten times the rate of that just across the border in Northumbria.

---

[1] These figures only cover the existing records and as such can give only an incomplete picture. What they do appear to show is that, even in the existing record, the Borders execution rate was higher than average.

2

The 17th century saw Scotland still reeling from the effects of the great religious wars of the Reformation. The Reformation that had swept Europe arrived in Scotland in various forms in the early 16th century. The beliefs of Luther and Calvin and their criticisms of the church were vigorously debated by many including John Knox. Knox' influence on the direction of the new church would be immense and the Protestant Reformation in Scotland would be Calvinist in its nature.

His attitudes towards both witches and women would also have a lasting legacy. His famous pamphlet *The First Blast of the Trumpet against the Monstrous Regiment of Women,* may have been aimed at women such as Mary Tudor and Mary Guise mother of Mary Queen of Scots but like all such documents it took on a life of its own and percolated into the psyche of many. The bastardized message was clear: power was not a state natural to women, that women would always seek power over men and subsequently those women who sought power were to be feared. Previous beliefs about women and their place in society were given a religious legitimacy. This message, in combination with other factors, would play its part in the preponderence of female victims brought to trial in Scotland. For Knox, witches were, with the Devil, quite simply the enemy of God and his people. The rooting out and execution of witches was, therefore, nothing less than war.

'For all those that would draw us from God (be they Kings or Quenes) being of the Devil's nature, are enemyis unto God, and therefore will God that in such cases we declare ourselves enemyis unto them'. (John Knox 1564)

In 1557 the Lords of the Congregation drew up their covenant to *'maintain, set forth, and establish the most blessed Word of God and his Congregation.'*. And in 1560 the Parliament convened in Edinburgh and set up a 'committee of the articles' which recommended a condemnation of papal authority, a restoration of early Church discipline and a redistribution of Church wealth to the ministry and the poor. It then approved a Reformed Confession of Faith and passed three Acts that destroyed the old Catholic faith in Scotland. Scotland was now a Protestant country.

One of the main changes in the Kirk was that candidates for the ministry were to be examined as to their suitability for the post of Minister and would be elected by the local congregation. The congregation would be led by a committee of Elders. Most Ministers would be elected from the committee. Power would, therefore, come to be concentrated in the hands of those Elders. The Kirk was also to engage in education. Education was to be established at all levels from village school to university and while this would lead to an increased literacy amongst the Scots, it was mainly used at a local level to teach communities the correct moral code by which to live.

And a new moral code was needed. Superstition remained and would prove to be a thorny issue for many years for the Kirk. The Christian faith had, in the early days, absorbed many pagan customs and practices understanding that in the matter of local customs a degree of leniency was a better method of gaining converts than coercion. But that had been the old Catholic faith Scotland was now a Calvinist nation and superstitions were now viewed as the remains of the old disgraced faith and had to be stamped out. Where before belief in kelpies and lucky charms had been part and parcel of life they were now viewed with increasing suspicion and disapproval.

There was also the matter of authority. The Kirk was the true keeper of the faith and old women in their cottages could not use charms to ensure a fertile marriage bed or a good harvest. God was not at the beck and call of old women, to presume to know the mind of God was blasphemous. And if their power did not come from God there was only one other place from which it could emanate, the Devil.

The Devil would prove a tenacious foe throughout the century as he sought to undermine the new faith. When Elizabeth of England finally died in 1603 and James VI gained the English throne few would have predicted that this would be the start of a turbulent century for both countries.

It was said by some that the King was glad to be quit of Scotland for her richer southern neighbour. And it is true that England was, by comparison with Scotland, a much richer nation but there were not a few that said James was also glad to be leaving a country where only thirteen years previously a coven of witches had tried to drown the king and his Danish bride at North Berwick.

Whatever the truth of the matter, James was only to return to his native land once between 1603 and his death in 1625. The rule of Scotland was left in the hands of the Parliament and the Kirk. James, busy with his new court life in London, diplomatically left the religion of the Scots to the Scots with the Presbyterian Kirk managing a reasonable co-existence with other faiths and forms.

His son, Charles I, was however less of a stateman than his father. His belief in the Divine Right of Kings was absolute and he was determined to make his mark. He had little love of his northern nation and visited rarely but what he did want was uniformity of faith over his entire Kingdom. This wish was to cost him dear.

In 1629, barely four years into his reign, he was governing without the Parliament in London. With no opposition to challenge him he started on his plans to reform his Kingdom. In 1637, Charles, failing to understand the place of the Kirk in Scottish society, decided, with the help of the Archbishop of Canterbury, William Laud, to impose the Anglican hierarchy and full liturgy on the Church in Scotland. In 1638 Scotland, understanding completely what the King was attempting to do, rioted and signed the National Covenant. The Covenant was taken round Scotland where many thousands signed including many in the Borders. Sworn to defend the faith a Covenanter army sprang up to oppose the King.

By 1639 the Covenanters had taken control of several Scottish towns including Edinburgh and Stirling while the General Assembly of the Kirk abolished episcopacy. Charles, outraged by the Scottish upstarts, was also alarmed by their number and in 1639 managed to broker an uneasy truce. Failing again to understand the mood of the Scots, Charles ignored the unspoken but implicit conditions of the truce and continued on with his reforms as before.

By 1640 the Covenanters, angered by the King's duplicity, were on the march down through the Borders to Newcastle. Charles summoned the Parliament in London for assistance. However, he was to be disappointed by a lukewarm response to his request and a list of unprecedented demands from the Parliamentarians in exchange for their support.

The Covenanters, clear in their aims to establish a Presbyterian Kirk in both Scotland and England, were, for differing reasons, courted by both King and Parliamentarians. They eventually made an alliance, the Solemn League and Covenant of 1643, pledging Scottish armies for the English Parliamentary cause in return for religious support. Borders men would be called to serve in the army. While the Covenanters believed the Solemn League and Covenant commited the Parliamentarians to the establishment of a national Presbyterian church both north and south of the border, the Parliamentarians did not favour Presbyterian rule.

The wars would rage over the whole of the United Kingdom and the Borders was no exception. In 1645 Royalist troops led by Montrose met with the Covenanters led by Leslie at Philiphaugh near Selkirk. The Covenanters defeated the Royalist army and Montrose fled the field. Many of the Irish foot soldiers, who had fought for Montrose, surrendered under the promise of quarter. Undaunted by this pledge of honour, several Kirk Ministers urged the Covenanters to put the Irish to the sword. This slaughter included the camp followers which comprised around three hundred women and children.

In 1646 Charles surrendered to the Scottish army at Newark. Unable to reach any agreement with the King, the army handed him over to the English. Politics continued to ebb and flow and in 1648 a Scots army invaded England this time on the King's behalf. The Covenanters, disappointed by the English Parliamentarians' lack of support for a unified Presbyterian faith, fought for Charles against Cromwell. In 1651 the Scots army was defeated at Worcester and in 1652 Scotland came under English Parliamentary rule.

For eight years, although chafing under English rules, the Borders remained free from battles. When Charles II was restored to the throne in 1660, the Kirk was re-established and a degree of stability was maintained. Disputes would arise from time to time but the fighting was, for the Borders, over.

In 1685 Charles' son James succeeded to the throne. James was a Catholic and his faith remained at odds with that of both Scotland and England. The Kirk waited to see how their new Catholic King would reign, would the Covenanters be recalled? James however had problems of his own to deal with in London and in 1689, after he had fathered a son and the threat of the establishment of a Catholic dynasty loomed, his daughter Mary, a Protestant, and her husband William were given the throne. The Protestant succession was secure. In 1690, the Kirk was formally given the Presbyterian form of government.

The century that was to see war was also to see plague and famine stalk the rural poor of the Borders again and again. The century started with an outbreak of plague, surely God's punishment for something. It was not an auspicious start. Plague not only affected those suffering the disease but, as a terrifying and unknown quantity, the respone to the cry of plague affected everyone. Almost all trade and communication came to a standstill. For a rural farming area dependent on the movement of farm goods to market, plague in Edinburgh and the Lothians may not have visited death on your doorstep but stopped trade. Unable to sell produce or move livestock the farming areas suffered.

Barely seven years later plague would reappear and this time came into the Border lands. Rumours of who had the plague ran through communities on the wind. No-one would buy your goods and no-one would sell you goods. Perfectly healthy, but suspected of plague, families could starve to death in their own homes unable to leave for fear of stoning or worse. There was nothing for it but to sit it out. Some survived, many did not.

And then, in 1623, the harvest failed throughout Scotland. The Borders with little or no food stored had to contend with riders from Edinburgh seeking to buy or steal what they needed for the hungry mouths in the capital. Hardy stock the Borderes survived just eking out their meagre rations over the year but even so the young and the old died. The next year brought no relief as plague returned. Those weakened by the previous year's starvation were easy prey and again the death toll rose.

The next year was better as was the following and Borderers cautiously rebuilt their lives. Year on year they remained plague free and the harvest was good. And then again in 1630 the call went up, plague. A smaller outbreak than the last but still some died, some fled and trade was badly affected. Once again Borderers somehow managed to pull through but in 1635 complete disaster struck. Plague and famine came together. For many it was too much and in many villages and towns entire families succumbed to the double blow. Farming, although unaffected by weather conditions over the next nine years, was slow to recover as the numbers of those left to work the land only slowly improved.

In 1644 it seemed as if God was truly punishing the Scots when yet again plague and famine came hand in hand into Borders towns and villages. Who was left to die?

Plague, at least, seemed to leave the Borders then and moved south to torment others but barely four years on in 1648 the harvest failed again and starvation pulled at the bellies of Border's children. Mortality rose to around one in three; a harsh lesson for many parents of young infants. Once more the young and the old died and once more trade was poor.

And then things appeared to lighten. Between 1649 and 1674 the weather remained benevolent with good crops and sheep and kye(cattle) that readily fattened. Trade was good and while wars still raged and religious disputes continued there was at least sufficient food. Then in 1675 the harvest failed again but memories had been long and much had been stored during the previous harvest while the previous good years meant that, for the main, folks were fitter than before and could withstand one bad year. And true enough 1676 saw another mild year with a good harvest and was followed by another and another.

In 1695 the harvest failed again and this was the start of seven years of starvation, famine and food shortages in the Borders. The old century was going out, as tainted as it had arrived.

Plague and famine had not been the only terrors to stalk the Borders. If the 17th century was the time of witch burnings, the 16th century was the time of the Reivers. The reiving families from both sides of the Borders rode out wreaking damage on rival families and innocent communities alike. Men were murdered, kye stolen and houses put to the torch. With no recognition of the Border or of the law on either side the Reivers rode with impunity. Disrespectful of the authority of either crown they knew only allegiance to their heidsman and family. Their society developed such that the authorities in Edinburgh and London came close to washing their hands of the entire region. Designated the 'debatable lands', wardens were posted to keep the peace with little hope of success and far less protection for local communities.

The union of the crowns saw the end of the reiving way of life but its influence would be felt in the Borders long into the 17th century. The Kirk knew full well the lack of respect that had been shown to the authorities by the reiving families and equally knew how insidious such a notion could be. The flagrant lack of respect offered to the law could also be shown to the Kirk. And it was that legacy that the Kirk feared.

In ordinary communities however, while the dawning of the new century appeared to offer the promise of no more nightly raids, no more burnings, how could they be sure? The authorities in Edinburgh had failed to protect them before and so when trouble struck Borderers knew better than to expect any help. In many Borders witch trials there was little contact with the authorities in Edinburgh except what was absolutely necessary. The Borders looked after its own.

An area that had seen wars, Reivers, plague and famine was truly one that was under attack by the Devil's own. An area unlike any other in Scotland. 1700 saw the arrival of the new century. A century that would see the union of the Parliaments and the flowering of the Scottish Enlightenment. In the Borders, 1700 saw the burning of Meg Lawson in the Gallows Knowe in Selkirk for the *'wicked cryme of witchcraft'*.

2. PEEBLES 1629

'vehementlie suspect of wytchcraft

eebles in the 17th century was a relatively prosperous town sitting as it did beside the river Tweed and one of the main trading roads to Edinburgh. Well off and well educated this was not a town that succumbed to the ignorant superstitions of its rural cousins, or so the people of Peebles confidently thought. The Minister of the town would talk of the witches caught further east and south in the Borders and warn his flock to be ever vigilant. But that was typical of the wild debatable lands of Reiver country, not of the lush green calm of Peebles. And then 1629 dawned, and that calm was broken. The summer brought fine weather and the promise of a good harvest but it also brought twenty seven accused witches to trial.

The spring had been soft that year and the nights pleasant and mild. After a long day's work folks had gathered in door ways and lanes to talk and pass the day's news. May blossom floated on the breeze as neighbour nodded to neighbour noting who was here and there. But evening chat started to turn to gossip as late night gatherings were seen. Why did Katherine Wode and Marion Boyd always hurry so down towards the Tor Hill? And why did Patrick Lintoun yawn all the morning when he should surely have been abed all night? Idle curiosity was fast becoming more substantial when Marion Boyd, Gilbert Hog and Janet Hendersoun missed the Kirk service two Sundays in a row. This sin of omission was further compounded when all three claimed illness and yet had been seen on both Sundays out on the drover's road.

It's not known exactly when the word witch was first uttered, or who first whispered it, but once mentioned, under the breath and with a cautious look over the shoulder, there could be no stopping the consequences. It was well know that last winter when many had been ill Bessie Ur and Margaret Gowanlock had tended to the sick. And then it was remembered that neither Bessie nor Margaret had fallen ill themselves but several they had tended had died. The neighbours of William Thomesoun now recalled a quarrel that had resulted in a lame horse. Accusations started to fly and so did some of the accused. Marion Crosier, Gilbert Hog and Margaret Dicksoun fled the town. More names were whispered and the Presbytery of Peebles met. The meeting lasted well into the night and when they rose the Moderator had a list of twenty seven names.

Agnes Chalmers, Sussanna Elphinstoun, Margaret Yerkine, William Thomesoun, William Mathesoun, Thomas Stoddart, Agnes Robesoun, Katherine Broun, Marie Johnestoun, Janet Hendersoun, Agnes Thomesoun, Katherine Wode, Marion Crosier, Issobel Haddock, Gilbert Hog, Jean Watsoun, Margaret Dicksoun, Margaret Johnestoun, Janet Achesoun, Bessie Ur, Katherine Alexander, Helen Beatie, Margaret Gowanlock, Marion Boyd, Katherine Mairschell, Patrick Lintoun and John Graham know as Joke the Graham. They were all noted to be *'vehementlie suspect of wytchcraft'*. Within the week a Commission had been received from the Privy Council in Edinburgh to the Baillies and Sheriffs of Peebles, Dalkeith and Glasgow to *'search for, apprehend, arrest and interrogate said accused persones'*. The interrogation to take place within fifteen days of the arrest.

The town was in an uproar, twenty seven had been named, not even the worst town gossips had guessed at that number. Doors were suddenly closed and evenings chats became a thing of the past. Attendance at the Kirk on Sunday was strictly adhered to by all even the sick. In the town the Sheriff deputised more men and the search began. Some had made it as far as Innerleithen and one, it is true, was apprehended on the road to Biggar but soon all were rounded up and the interrogations began. The charges were similar in all cases, that they had met at night for nefarious purposes, that they had made a compact with the Devil and denied their baptism. That they had frolicked with the Devil and that he had helped them to lay sickness on various neighbours some of whom had died as a resulted. All twenty seven denied all the charges.

And then the questioning began. Day after day, night after night. The Baillie's men working in shifts round the clock, the accused allowed no sleep, no respite from the constant threats and intimidation. The Elders quoting texts, bullying and harrying. Issobel Haddock, described as a young girl, was the first to confess. Yes she had gone to a meeting on the Tor Hill, yes the Devil was there, yes there were others there, yes she knew them, yes she would name them. The ultimate proof: she would name them. And with the first confession came all the others tumbling over each other to tell what they had done, what they had said, and who they had seen. Shrieking agreement to whatever question was put to them; Sheriff's men were posted outside the Tolbooth to keep the curious away. The trial date was set for 11 June.

The big room of the Tolbooth was crowded even before the accused were brought in. The jury of townsmen of good character, selected by the Presbytery, sat together on a double row of wooden benches. While the Kirk Elders sat before a table containing several manuscripts. Another table was occupied by the prosecutors and a third by the court clerk. The back of the room was filled with various townsfolk while down at the front were a number of low stools. There were not enough stools for all of the accused to sit down and some were forced to sit on the stone floor. Some were weeping, some sat dejected, others seemed oblivious to the whole affair playing with the ends of their hair or staring vacantly around them at the curious spectators. The Minister rose and facing the assembled crowd read out the charges and confessions. No defence was offered by any of the accused.

The speed with which the accused had gone from being free men and women to being arrested, charged, interrogated and tried seemed to have rendered them unable to contemplate even a token protest. The trial was over in a day with verdicts and sentences an almost foregone conclusion. When the Minister rose to speak it was with the inevitable list of Agnes Chalmers guilty, sentenced to death, Patrick Lintoun, guilty, sentenced to death, Margaret Yerkine, guilty, sentenced to death until twenty four names had been called. Sussanna Elphinstoun, Margaret Johnestoun and Joke the Graham were not named. They were found not proven and returned to the keeping of the Baillie until their fate was decided. Five days later their twenty four colleagues were walked, barefoot and bareheaded, up to the Calf Knowe, worriet and then burnt in tar barrels. From arrest to execution had taken less than 21 days.

The next session of the Presbytery however, was not a contented one. If twenty four were guilty how could the other three be innocent? The not proven verdicts were set aside and the Presbytery applied to the Privy Council for a further Commission. Until the Commission was received, Sussanna, Margaret and Joke the Graham were kept in custody. Unluckily for them the Privy Council was busy with Commissions for several other Borders towns and they sat out the summer and autumn incarcerated awaiting a second trial.

By the time the Commission was finally received it was December and the trial was held on the 22 of the month. On this occasion the guilty verdicts of the former twenty four was used as further evidence against Sussanna, Margaret and Joke the Graham as was the fact of their imprisonment since the summer. The implication was clear, innocent persons do not have executed witches for friends and do not get locked up by the authorities for six months without just cause. As before the trial lasted only a day with the former trial's jury having been brought back to correct their previous mistaken verdict. On this occasion all three were found guilty and sentenced to death. The order was sent again to the Baillie and his men, *'prepare them for death'*. They were worriet and burnt on Christmas Eve with the Minister leading his flock directly from the execution site to the Kirk for the midnight service to celebrate Christ's birth.

During the 17th century the Presbyterian Kirk in Scotland was struggling to assert itself and define its final form. The young faith was in danger from all sides as the Devil used all his wiles to attack them. Not content with giving succour to those stubbornly remaining Catholic in their beliefs and aiding and abetting royalist plots to force a common prayer book upon them, the Devil also used the common people. Preying upon their ignorance and superstition, he ensnared them into his service and a plague of witches was unleashed upon the land. Under attack the General Assembly passed their Condemnatory Acts against witches in 1640, 1643, 1644, 1645 and 1649.

The Border's Presbyteries suffered the same trials and tribulations as the rest of Scotland as they struggled to find their feet against a backdrop of war, famine and plague. Truly they were under attack and whilst this served to prove to them the rightness of their path it also called upon them to fight for their very souls against those forces that sought to destroy them. Catholics, Kings and covens of witches all would prove to be formidable foes but all would ultimately be defeated.

The new faith was the true faith and yet there were those that stubbornly refuse to accept this. In the eyes of many, Catholic resistance was more than just a refusal to accept a new form of worship it was an affront to God and as such must be inspired by the Devil. Rituals and incantations muttered in Latin and the mysteries of the mass became to be thought of as having more than a whiff of brimstone about them. The fresh ideals of the Reformation quickly became bogged down into mistrust and hatred as the remaining Catholics clung tenaciously to their faith.

The Borders held few Catholics but paradoxically their scarcity merely heightened the conviction that their beliefs were superstitious in the extreme. This in turn influenced the perceptions of the authorities of any behaviour not totally sanctioned by Kirk.

The Protestant establishment, determined to destroy the Catholic faith in Scotland, or at the very least break its power, described Catholic beliefs as superstition. The Witchcraft Act of 1563 outlawed superstition and superstitious practices by the people, but it was left to the Kirk to define those superstitions. Known Catholics with their beliefs were easily identified, but what about those who merely followed the beliefs handed down to them by grandparents. Belief in curses or lucky amulets stemmed from older pagan times but remained strong nonetheless. And what about those women known to make herbs and potions? Called on in times of childbirth or when illness struck a family: theirs was a precarious position. Ordinary people in local communities had long believed in lucky charms and herbal remedies, were these now superstition? Was lucky white heather or a nailed horseshoe over a door way now suspect? Unfortunately there was no proscribed list of outlawed practices and the interpretation was left in the hands of the local Minister.

While witchcraft affected all of Scotland it is noticeable that in the Highlands and Islands the Gaelic culture allowed for a much more lenient interpretation of what was superstition and subsequently witchcraft trials were an infrequent event. The Border's Presbyteries however, saw the Devil and all his works at every turn and in every gesture. Fully in control of village schools they determined the moral code and those stepping outside those boundaries would not be viewed with Gaelic indulgence but with lowland suspicion.

The domestic world, the domain of women, was an area where women held authority. That sat uneasily with the Kirk and its teachings. Dominated by men whose views on women were typical of Europe at the time, these teachings would have horrific consequences. While men were sometimes arrested and tried as witches the majority of those accused were women. In Scotland, as a whole, around 84% of those suspected were women, in the Borders the figure was even higher at 92% of known cases. But why should this be? Why were women believed to be witches in such large numbers? The reason goes back to early beliefs anent women and their inferiority to and difference from men.

The *Malleus Maleficarum*, the great guide to witches and their ways, written by Heinrich Institoris in 1486, outlined in detail why women were more susceptible to witchcraft. The *Malleus* started with the statement that there was no point offering the opinion that there were not more female witches than male as it was patently true by anyone and everyone's observation. After this opening certainty, the book outlined, at great length, the reasons why. It was a commonly held belief that women did not know how to be moderate in their goodness or their wickedness and when they passed the boundaries of their proper status they became extremely wicked. Institorus, the author of the *Malleus* quoted various sources for this belief, from Roman historians such as Seneca to Christian scholars such as St Augustine and then finally the scriptures themselves.

Institoris

Heinrich Institoris was born around 1430 in Schlettstadt on the border of modern day Germany and France. He trained for the church and gained a reputation as as impressive lecturer in theology. Known for his passionate beliefs, he served time in gaol for defamatory remarks he made during a sermon about the Holy Roman Emperor Frederick III. After his release he was made Dominican inquisitor for the province of Teutonia.

Around 1460 he went to Rome to continue his studies. His time there was marred with at least one street brawl. On his return to Schlettstadt he became involved in a conflict with a local priest and was arrested on the orders of Pope Sixtus IV for theft and lost his position. He managed to redeem himself and regained his position as inquisitor. He spent the next few years travelling and investigating cases of heresy and witchcraft.

In 1485, he arrived in Innsbruck becoming involved in the witchcraft trial of fifty women.Institoris believed witchcraft was a reality, the local Bishop, Georg Golser, however, thought witchcraft was an illusion caused by evil spirits. These different beliefs were to prove insurmountable. Institoris investigated the allegations against the women thoroughly including using torture and close questioning about the sexual behaviour of the women.The Bishop objected to Institoris' methods and appointed an overseer for the trials who was more disposed to the Bishop's views.

When the trial started Institoris' investigations, and thus the evidence resulting from them, was ruled inadmissable.The women were acquitted. Institoris was both humiliated and angry and had to leave Innsbruck under threat of violence.

In 1486 he wrote the Malleus Maleficarum. The book was intended to instruct legal authorities how to prosecute witches. As witchcraft was, by its very nature, a largely unseen crime and as witches with the help of the Devil were both tricky and deceitful, prosecuting them was fraught with difficulties as the trial at Innsbruck had shown. The Malleus was Institoris' attempt to help others with this tricky problem as well as a defence of his own beliefs.

The book is long and complex dealing not only with witches and how to identify and prosecute them but, no doubt as a rebuke to Bishop Golser, also discusses those who lack the mettle to pursue witches with extreme and steadfast purpose. Controversial to the last Institoris forged a letter of recommendation about the Malleus from the University of Cologne resulting in another court case against him.

In his later years he withdrew from witchcraft trials and spent his time writing manuscripts on theology. He died in 1505.

The Malleus Maleficarum remained the reference book on witchcraft for many years and, despite being written by a Catholic, would continue to do so even after the Reformation in both Protestant and Catholic countries alike.

It was also commonly believed that women were inclined to be gullible and naive and were thus easier to trick than men. The Devil, whose main aim was to destroy the true faith, would then use women as they were more trusting. And again Institorus quoted scripture to prove his point. Not only were women trusting but their bodies leaked. Menstrual blood and breast milk were the sure signs of a leaky and thus weak vessel. This made them more impressionable and so evil spirits could use them. Another problem with women was that they had a *'lewd and slippery'* tongue.

As if this were not enough women were also thought to be extremely lustful and given to carnal filthiness. This was supposed to have derived from women being created from Adam's rib. It was thought that as the part of the rib used has curved away from Adam's body it had left women unfinished and so weak and depraved and given to deceit. The derivation of the word *femina* was used to support this idea, as Institorus explained, that *fe* meant faith and *minus* meant less therefore women had less faith than men. What faith they did have they were less able to keep. According to the beliefs of the day a wicked woman, because of her poor character, would waver in her belief and would both quickly and easily deny her faith and this denial was the very foundation of her witchcraft.

Women were also castigated for their basic character. It was believed that women, when they hated someone they had previously loved, seethed and raged with hatred. This emotional excess made them seek revenge on anyone who had wronged them. They were also thought to have a defective memory and were impulsive and had a lack of duty. Even a woman's voice was likened to the deadly song of the sirens, able to kill men and make them deny God. The *Malleus* stated the fears about women and authority that Knox would pursue some seventy years later. If women were in control of men then disaster would strike. Their gait, posture and dress were designed to seduce men. They were also carnal and lustful and were never sexually satisfied: this inability to be satisfied led them to arouse themselves with evil spirits.

And what of women who were witches, what was believed of them? It was generally believed that three main vices held sway in women and even more so in wicked woman. They had a lack of faith, were licentious, and had self interest. The logic of the day stated that women applied themselves to witchcraft more than men because, unlike men, they were prey to those particular vices. Licentiousness was considered to be the most dominant of the vices. Selfish women were most deeply infected with evil if they also had uncontrollable lust.

The Kirk, like most churches of the time, seemed obsessed by females and sex and seven kinds of evil magic were listed by the church which involved sex in one form or other.

The first was by magically making people want excessive sex. It was generally believed that men were weak where sex was concerned and that women could and did entice them into having excessive sex. The church authorities were concerned that men would become blinded by lust and neglect their duties both spiritual and temporal.

Next was causing impotency. This was a huge concern to the church and to society as a whole. Impotent men could not father children, or more importantly sons, and as this was considered to be a non natural state had to be the result of witchcraft.

The third kind of evil magic was even worse. Shrinking or removing men's penises. This was a belief strongly held by ordinary people. Witches were thought to beguile men by offering extreme pleasure the price for which was the actual loss of manhood. The next was changing people into animals for sexual purposes.

The fifth type of magic was making women barren and the next was causing miscarriages. These were the two charges that were frequently laid at the door of midwives. As childbearing was the natural order of things a married woman who did not have children or who miscarried was believed to have been bewitched.

The last was sacrificing small children to the Devil. This macabre crime could either be carried out by killing a child and using its body or by digging up an existing dead child. In either case body parts, most notably bones, were offered to the Devil and sometimes ground up for use in ointments or in rituals.

That the faith was under attack was not in doubt. That women were potentially wicked was not in doubt. Putting the two together, the Borders Kirk had cause and effect identified and thus looked no further. But Borders witches were to face one more blow against them and that was the belief amongst many in the Kirk that the more Godly the Kirk the greater the ferocity of the Devil's attack. This became a self fulfilling prophesy in the Borders Presbyteries. The more Godly the Minister the more witches there would be in any local community. With the Kirk in control of the investigations into suspected witches the number could only increase. Equally as Ministers led the interrogation of suspected witches then the fate of those witches became in most cases a foregone conclusion. The presence of a witch proved how Godly the local Minister was and, obviously, how truthful when he called a suspect a witch: the truthfulness of the Minister proved the witch to be guilty.

The greater the number of witches in a community, the greater its Godliness. For why else would the Devil attack them? While the Kirk fought the Devil and all his followers it was local communities that suffered. Taught in their village schools what the moral code was, lectured from the pulpit on the dangers of women and surrounded and attacked by plague, famine and war, local comunities had only one saviour and that was the Kirk.

In the Border records that exist the same names reappear time and time again, Hume, Pringle, Scott, Veitch, Cleland. Men that were uncompromising in their faith, men that would, in their time, face gaol rather than accept anything less than a pure Presbyterian faith. These were men that investigated and interrogated witches not only in their own parishes but in neighbouring communities and further afield. They would travel the length and breadth of the Borders to help their brother Ministers in their times of trouble, helping to consign to the flames the witches that threatened their Kirk.

The Borders Kirk, proud inheritors of the independent Borders spirit, had seen their communities attacked by the Devil and knew their time had come. They were God's elect and this was their mission to drive witches from the face of the earth. Their zeal would consign two hundred and eighteen to the flames, others would die in gaol from their torture and treatment and still others would commit suicide.

Put to the horn

To be put to the horn was to be be denounced as a rebel. It meant the loss of name and status for the individual. It also placed the miscreant literally outside the law. This removal of the protection of the law thus gave everyone else the freedom to attack, imprison and even kill the individual with impunity.

Originally this punishment had started as a means of enforcing debtors to pay their creditors. Rather than face gaol, a debtor would pledge an oath before God to pay his debts. If the debtor broke his oath he became liable to the discipline of the Kirk as an oath breaker or perjurer. The civil authorities would then issue letters of horning denouncing the individual as a rebel. The messenger-at-arms would go to the Cross of Edinburgh and give three blasts with a horn before heralding the judgment of outlawry.This could result in the imprisonment of a named individual and the confiscation of his goods.

As time went on refusal to answer a court summons, which was issued in the name of the King, was also considered to be the breaking of an oath and thus would result in the individual being put to the horn.

It was frequently used against the Border Reivers. Individuals thought guilty of various offences would be summoned before a Sheriff to answer for their behaviour. Refusal to comply with the summons was tantamount to contempt of the King's authority and would result in the individual being declared outlaw.

3. DUNS 1630

'petition the king'

arket day in Duns December 1628 was abuzz with gossip about the goings on up in Haddington. Some vagabond had been arrested as a warlock and had named his witches. Ten had been named, twenty, thirty, day after day the story grew in the telling. Well what could be expected of a beggar from East Lothian, they bred witches up there that tried to drown Kings. As the new year dawned more and more strange tales would filter down from the farmers and drovers that plied their trade between Duns and Haddington. One year on from the initial arrest however, the good folk of Duns market would hear an accusation that would astound the whole of Berwickshire.

Duns was one of several market towns in the county of Berwickshire in the early 1600s. Created a Burgh of Barony in 1489, the town held a weekly market on a Tuesday and once a month this was expanded as livestock were driven into the market square to be bought and sold. Sitting in the lush green of Berwickshire farmland Duns held the usual Borders mix of properous local nobility, tenant farmers and farm labourers, merchants dealing in wool and grain and the familiar rag tag of the poor and the destitute in the back streets of the town. Market day would see them all rubbing shoulders, some to trade, more to gossip. The coming year would not disappoint.

Alexander Hammiltoun lived with his wife in Haddington East Lothian. Described variously as a vagabond and a beggar he would regularly desert his wife to go wandering about the countryside in search of easy pickings. Said to be from Newcastle, he wandered the back roads of East Lothian and the Berwickshire coast. From Tweedmouth and Berwick up to Prestonpans and occasionally inland to places such as Duns.

As the winter of 1628 started to bite Alexander started to walk back to Haddington begging as he went. Somewhere in the flatlands of East Lothian he had asked for alms and been refused. Alexander, tired and hungry, walked away with an ill grace muttering under his breath. Perhaps he spoke more loudly and aggressively then he intended, perhaps the householder had simply had their fill of beggars. Whatever the reason, Alexander, already a marginal and thus suspicious character, was arrested. A torrent of accusations quickly followed aided in no small part by Alexander himself who seemed keen to co-operate with the authorities naming several local women and detailing their activities over the previous four years.

Laying sickness, ruining crops, signing a pact with the Devil there seemed no end to Hammiltoun's wickedness. A self confessing witch he should have been brought to trial relatively quickly but by December 1629, almost one whole year since his initial arrest, he was still sitting in Haddington Tolbooth answering questions. Hammiltoun, no doubt due to the extent of his accusations, had several investigators involved in his case. One of them was Sir George Hume of Manderstoun. Hume interrogated Hammiltoun long and hard over the many months of his incarceration as the pact with the Devil and acts of witchcraft were detailed. The final confession however, would astound all. Hammiltoun named Helen Arnot, Lady Manderstoun and the wife of Sir George, as a witch.

According to Hammiltoun, Helen Arnot had come to him and asked him to help her ruin her husband's estate. Hammiltoun claimed to have resisted her and refused to help. After further questioning he admittted that she had called on him again and this time asked for his help to murder her husband.

Duns had never heard the like before. Neither had the local Kirk. Terrified by the prospect of offending a member of the nobility, but even more so of the unthinkable notion that she might be a witch, they quickly ensured that the case was sent to the Privy Council up in Edinburgh. No-one, it seems, wanted to deal with this case. Sir George was an investigator and now his own wife had been named for trying to kill him.

On 3 December 1629, the Privy Council drew up the order for the witnesses to Hammiltoun's statement about Lady Manderstoun to give evidence. William Mowat and Patrick Abernathy were investigators in the proceedings against Hammiltoun and had witnessed and recorded his accusations anent Helen. Both Mowat and Abernathy were servants of another of the trial investigators, James Mowat of Fawside. Mowat of Fawside was a writer to the signet. The Society of Writers to His Majesty's Signet was formed in 1594 and comprised only eighteen solicitors authorised to use the private seal of the king and to act as clerks to the courts. This was an extremely privileged position.

Lady Manderstoun denied all charges against her declaring them to be *'false and malicious'*. She is also said to have refused to appear before the court and to have threatened to have the court messenger whipped if she ever saw him again. Wiser counsel prevailed and nobody was whipped but on her arrest she demanded that Hammiltoun repeat his accusation before her.

With powerful friends Lady Manderstoun was not going to meekly submit to a trial and managed to get the Privy Council to send for Mowat and Abernathy to give evidence about the accusation.

Mowat and Abernathy failed to appear and within the week were put to the horn. Two weeks later the Privy Council repeated their order for Mowat and Abernathy to come forward and give evidence.

Christmas was a bleak time for all that year: Lady Manderstoun remained under arrest suspected of witchcraft, Mowat of Fawside faced explaining why his two servants had refused to give evidence and Alexander Hammiltoun still lay in Haddington Tolbooth. The Privy Council were worried. Was Lady Manderstoun a witch? If she was not, then who was lying, Sir George or a writer to the Signet? Unthinkable. There was no apparent solution that was not damaging. Unable to find an answer the Privy Council tried to pass the buck. Writing to the King and presuming on his great knowledge, after all his father had written the Scottish book on witchcraft, *Daemonologie*, they begged the King to intervene. Charles, busy ruling on his own after having dismissed his Parliament, failed to respond. They would have to deal with the situation themselves.

By the first week in January Mowat and Abernathy gave themselves up and confessed all. Yes they had heard Hammiltoun accuse Lady Manderstoun, yes he had been tortured and yes both Mowat of Fawside and Sir George had questioned Hammiltoun privately before his confession. The Privy Council had heard enough, William Mowat and Patrick Abernathy were both prosecuted for making false testimony against Lady Manderstoun.

Next to appear before the Privy Council was Hammiltoun. Brought from Haddington to Duns to be questioned he soon retracted his confession. He denied knowing Lady Manderstoun and that she had ever approached him to aid in the murder of her husband. Dismissed he was sent back to the Tolbooth in Haddington to await the outcome of the remaining charges against him. The Privy Council however had greater problems with which to wrestle. The confession of a vagabond warlock against that of Lady Manderstoun had been the height of impudence in the first place and its retraction was a welcome resolution. However, that left them with the question of who had pressured Hammiltoun to confess against her and why. They also had the problem that Mowat and Sir George remained the lead investigators in the Hammiltoun case. To remove them from the case implied they were guilty; to investigate them while the case was ongoing was risky. The Council decided on the lesser of two evils and Mowat and His Lordship continued to preside over the vagabond's case until its completion in the following January.

All charges against Lady Manderstoun were formally dropped on the 2 February. An investigation into the reasons behind the orginal accusation was instigated and Mowat of Fawside was arrested and put to the horn for lying about Hammiltoun's deposition against Lady Manderstoun. In July however, the Privy Council rescinded the order against him. In 1631 charges of fabricating confessions were brought against Mowat of Fawside in another witchcraft case. Found proven he was arrested but managed to escape imprisonment.

In late 1630 Sir George had to petition the Privy Council for protection against his creditors. He claimed the expenses he had incurred during the Hammiltoun case were a drain upon his purse. No charges were ever laid against him anent his wife and Hammiltoun's confession.

In the original confession about Lady Manderstoun, Hammiltoun claimed to have introduced her to the Devil and that they had all had communal sex. He also claimed that they had taken part in a ritual, using a dead fowl, to bewitch Sir George to death. This had taken place in a barn on Sir George's land. What was the most damning was obvious. What was the most scandalous however, was the idea of a lady of the nobility, who was of child bearing age and could thus produce an heir, having intercourse with a vagabound. Innocent of the charges she might have been, innocent of the act was another matter.

It was never statisfactorily established who, if anyone, had coerced Hammiltoun into naming Lady Manderstoun. Had he been induced to name her, as some thought? Or was she indeed a witch and had lain with Hammiltoun to induce him to kill her husband? Hammiltoun's retraction came after the Privy Council had spoken to Mowat and Abernathy. Had he sensed how the wind had changed and altered his story accordingly?

The decisions of the Privy Council in this case were a balancing act between determining the truth and offending powerful members of the nobility. The decision not to interview Hammiltoun until after Mowat and Abernathy had been seen was never questioned. What can be gleaned from the records is that at the time at least two members of the Privy Council were related to the Arnot family.

On 10 November 1632 Lady Manderstoun scandalised Berwickshire once again by divorcing her husband. Proof, it was said, of her wickedness and ungodliness. It was also said that her husband was glad to be rid of such as her. Alexander Hammiltoun's fate remains unknown.

Human culture moves slowly and at different speeds for different peoples. It is not tidy and does not fit neatly into nicely labelled time periods. Beliefs and behaviours spill over from one time to another and may mix and evolve over the centuries. This is true for many aspects of human culture including the spiritual. The Borders has been populated since around 6500 BC and the evidence from the earliest times suggests that these early Borderers worshipped a 'Horned God'. While various peoples arrived as settlers or invaders the pagan religion remained relatively unchanged for several centuries. The first Christians arrived around the fifth century. However, even after Christianity established itself the two beliefs co-existed for some considerable time. As the centuries wound on, Christianity became more dominant with more and more of the ruling orders becoming Christian while most ordinary folk continued to worship the old gods.

The main point of contention was the Christian separation of good and evil into two different entities while the pagan religion contenting itself with a duality within their gods. This duality was of both intent and gender. The Christians however, being monotheistic, believed any non Christian deity to be a devil. While a female god was just unthinkable. Friction increased. Previous peaceful co-existence was wearing thin. When the Reformation occurred religion and politics became intertwined as the ruling classes predominantly adopted the new religion while Catholicism was left with the lower orders who, although nominally Christian, still carried out and believed in many pagan rituals. As the Reformation progressed in Scotland and more and more people converted to the Protestant faith they simply brought their pagans beliefs with them.

Those beliefs was expressed in many ways but were dominated by death. Death was a common visitor in the many rural areas of Scotland including the Borders through illness, wars or famine. The pagan religion offered a method of articulating fears and dealing with the spirits of the dead. The Protestant faith failed to provide a similar method of understanding and comfort. The spirits of the dead had to be appeased to protect the living from their anger and to ease their passage into the other world. Catholics masses for the dead would tread dangerously close to this old belief proving to the Protestant clergy, if proof were needed, that Catholics, pagans and witches were all the same. Halloween would prove to be a tenacious relic from those days.

Halloween

Halloween originated in the Celtic festival of Samhain. Regarded as the Celtic New Year it was a celebration of the end of harvest. But it was also the time when the boundaries between the world of the living and the world of the dead faded away allowing the dead to pass from their realm to the world of the living. It was the time of the year when the living honoured the dead and paid their respects to departed family members. Tales were told of the heroism and battles that the departed had undertaken and won. This is probably the origin of the modern tradition of telling ghost stories at this time.

A great feast would be prepared which involved the slaughter of livestock and their bones would be thrown onto the bone-fire (bonfire). However not all the spirits that returned were friendly so faces would be blacked and costumes worn to hide from spirits thought to have evil intent.

Try as it might the Christian church could not shake this festival. But what it could and did do was to demonise the original horned god. The lack of understanding from the Kirk and the intransigence of ordinary people made any accommodation impossible. As far as the Christian fathers were concerned, the Horned God was simply the Devil by another name. A belief in the Horned God was therefore worship of the Devil. For ordinary folk however, while the Horned God faded from memory and became conflated with the Devil, the surrounding beliefs remained.

The Kirk believed that witches were in league with the Devil: that they had renounced their Christianity and made a pact or covenant with the Devil. Ordinary people however, did not think in such formalised terms. Carrying a lucky amulet was not seen by Borders villagers as anti Christian, but merely a normal activity albeit a cultural throwback to the old Horned God. Ordinary people were able to accommodate their Christianity and their superstition. The Kirk was not.

What had previously been tolerated by the Catholic Church was anathema to the new Presbyterian Kirk. Practises that had been innocently pursued were now castigated and given a diabolical basis. In the early days of the Kirk's witch hunts people confessed, not because they were mad or confused or even tortured. They confessed that yes they had left an offering to the man with the black hat or had looked in water to find stolen property. These were the common activities of most people. While some were, no doubt, witches, in the eyes of both themselves and their neighbours, the vast majority were just ordinary people with superstitious beliefs. Their confessions were true. It was simply that what was a normal procedure for them had become an act of evil to the Kirk.

While many did confess to making a pact with the Devil, care must be taken over this. Some of those who confessed to a covenant with the Devil did genuinely believe that they had met the Devil, the remnant of the old horned god. However, it must be remembered that the fervent beliefs of the interrogators led them to try to discover a diabolic element to witch craft and frame their questioning accordingly. What needs to be clearly understood is that they were not manipulating the questions to get the answers they wanted but were stressing the questions that they felt would allow them to get at the real truth of the matter. The Devil and his works. When witches said they made a covenant with the Devil this was not Devil worship as a cult, an alternative religious belief to Christianity, it was more a pact between one person and the Devil himself. The old horned god had been a god with whom an individual could bargain, combined with the new aspect of personal responsibility, introduced by the Protestant reformers, witches were damned for their choice of god and their method of interaction with him which mocked the Covenant with the Presbyterian God.

Witch's confessions were not fevered overblown tales of Gothic horror but were much more mundane and more horrific for that. They were the confessions of women and men sometimes lonely, usually poor, who believed they had met the Devil who had made them promises of power over their enemies or ample food for the winter. They made a covenant with the Devil and got revenge on those who had slighted them. A neighbour, who years previously has refused to help, would lose a cow. An unpaid debt would see ale soured. These simple stories show the horror of how ordinary life could be so easily subverted. There was little if any flying around and certainly no flying on broomsticks or turning your neighbour into a toad. These were everyday matters: causing the milk of a neighbour's cow to dry up, spoiling ale, raising a storm to ruin crops. But what started as a neighbourhood quarrel could all too soon descend into darker waters. Sickness laid on a child and the murder of an enemy with no apparent risk of capture was too easy a lure to reject. Homeliness and horror in equal measure.

The Devil's work was a serious business and witches rarely if ever had time for frivolities concentrating on life and death matters such as the weather, crops, kye, illness and fertility. It is rare in any of the trial records to hear of witches being promised or seeking after great riches. These were years of food shortages and war. You were much more likely to survive through the winter with your kye alive and healthy than with a hoard of gold beneath your bed.

While most 17th century Scots were merely superstitious there were those who were known as and believed themselves to be witches. Turned to by their neighbours in times of trouble they used their craft in ways that threatened Kirk authority. While the Kirk believed in a supernatural being who would reward you for worshipping him and following his code of behaviour, witches believed in a supernatural being who would reward them for worshipping him and following his code of behaviour. Unfortunately for the witches, their supernatural being was the wrong one.

The religious and superstitious beliefs of most ordinary people in the 17th century were no different from their beliefs of the 16th century or for that matter of the beliefs they would hold in the 18th century. What was to prove fatal however, was the inability of the Kirk to accept any deviation from the proscribed dogma of the day, and the inability of ordinary folk to dissemble. It has been suggested that one of the reasons why the nobility were rarely arrested for witchcraft was not that they did not believe in witches and witchcraft; it was rather that they were better liars and better able to hide their superstitious beliefs behind a façade of Christian respectability than the ordinary folk of the Borders.

It is likely that of all those arrested for witchcraft some would, no doubt, have described themselves as witches, the vast majority however were ordinary people trying to survive in a harsh world the best they could. But whether witch or not almost all were innocent of the charges brought against them.

4. EYEMOUTH 1634

'the devil be in your feet'

Known locally as a small fishing village but better known the length of Berwickshire as the haunt of smugglers and rogues, Eyemouth would, like other Borders towns, see many witches condemned to the flames in the 17th century. However in 1634 a trial was held that would expose the form of justice administered by the local Kirk and nobility and how, with some money, it was possible to challenge that justice.

Eight women and men were arrested for witchcraft. At least four would be put to death and two more would commit suicide; one, Elizabeth Bathgate, would walk free after an acquittal in Edinburgh.

Elizabeth was a 57 year old native of Eyemouth. She was married to a maltman and as such was reasonably well off. The charges against her seem to have arisen as a result of a series of disputes with several neighbours. One, George Sprot, had borrowed some cloth from Elizabeth. After George had held onto the cloth for longer than Elizabeth had expected, she demanded the return of the cloth while cursing him. A few days later she visited his house when he was out and after nipping his young child, left behind an egg. The child grew ill with an egg shaped lump on its body and then died.

She was alleged to have crippled William Donaldsoune by calling out *'the devil be in your feet'* when he ran from her. She laid a sickness

on John Gray's bairn. She had a long running feud with Margaret
Home who frequently borrowed money from Elizabeth's husband.
Elizabeth cursed Margaret on at least three separate occasions, killing
one horse, sending another mad and killing an ox. She was accused
of laying a sickness on Steven Allan and of killing David Hynd. What
was more serious however were the accusations of her dealings with
the Devil and other witches.

These events and others such as the burning of a local mill caused
the authorities to act and several local suspects were arrested and
interrogated and statements were taken. Several names were given
to the authorities including that of Elizabeth.

Two local men swore they had seen her talking to a man in green
clothes they thought was the Devil. Elizabeth was dressed only in her
sark at the time and when they had spoken to her she had ignored
them and one man told the other of her bad reputation saying '*her name
is not lucky*'. This was followed by an accusation that the Devil had
given her a horseshoe which she had buried at the Devil's instruction
and with the understanding that if she did as he bid she would never
want for money. She was named by several other suspected witches
as having been with them at a meeting with the Devil presiding and
later when they had destroyed a mill. They also named her as one of
the group that had sunk George Hurdie's boat. One of the witches,
William Mearns, described as a notorious warlock, stated that she
was a witch and had been at several witch assemblies at which the
Devil had presided. A second witch, Margaret Ballanie, also named
Elizabeth calling her a '*sicker witch*' than herself.

While this was a longer than usual list of complaints, it was the
normal litany of offences and included all eight other accused. In 1633
papers were lodged against, Alison Wilson, Agnes Wilson, Elspeth
Wilson, Williams Mearns, Margaret Ballanie in Aytoun, Patrick
Smith, Jennet Williamson and Elizabeth Bathgate. All were rounded
up and incarcerated. For some reason that remains unclear, Elizabeth
Bathgate was sent to the Tolbooth in Duns while the others were all

incarcerated in Eyemouth. It may be that Elizabeth was considered more dangerous than the others and had to be separated from them or it could have been a more prosaic reason. Elizabeth was the last to be arrested so there may simply not have been sufficient room left in Eyemouth gaol.

Whatever the reason Elizabeth did not take too kindly to her imprisonment and on the 16 December 1633 she lodged a complaint with the Privy Council against Sir Patrick Hume of Ayton and Mr John Hume Minister of Eyemouth for illegally imprisoning her on a charge of witchcraft. Elizabeth Bathgate was no helpless victim. This was the first of four complaints she made to the Privy Council.

On the 9 January 1634 she complained again about her false imprisonment. On the 11 February she was moved to Edinburgh Tolbooth in preparation for her trial. The pre trial preparation took longer than expected and on 11 February Elizabeth complained about this and the financial hardship that maintaining her in prison was costing her family. On the 27 February she lodged her final complaint that witness depositions that had been taken outwith her presence, and not in a court of justice, were going to be offered into evidence in her trial. This final compliant although in Elizabeth's name probably emanated from her legal team. The statements were disallowed unless the deponers came to Edinburgh to ratify them. Elizabeth then petitioned for release from prison pending the actual trial. She asked for a warrant to remain in Edinburgh which was granted. She was released from the Tolbooth in Edinburgh on 11 March.

On the 4 of June 1634 the Lord Advocate and Sir Patrick Hume brought their case against Elizabeth in Edinburgh. Eighteen different counts were laid against her and, as at least two other named witches had 'delated' or named her as a witch, her chances were not good. However Elizabeth did have a strong defence team that consisted of Robert Burnet, defence advocate, Laurence MacGill, defence advocate, David Prymrois, defence advocate and Alexander Pae.

The charges against Elizabeth were; Murder of George Sprot's child by nipping and using an enchanted egg, causing George Sprot to become poor, crippling William Donaldson, laying a sickness on John Gray's bairn, killing Margaret Homes' horse, killing Margaret Homes' ox, making Margaret Homes' horse mad, damaging George Auchterlonie's barn, conjuring and running widdershins on the mill, taking to the Devil in her shift, being delated a witch by Margaret Ballanie, burning the mill at Eyemouth with other witches, burying a horseshoe the Devil had given her, being delated a witch by William Mearns a warlock, sinking George Huldie's ship with other witches and after being confronted by these other witches being delated by them.

The charges were both serious and numerous and her defence team set about having as many of the charges as possible dropped before the trial began. They started on the charge of having sunk George Hurdie's ship. This was a serious charge, not least because it would raise memories in many of the North Berwick witches who had tried to drown the King by raising a storm to sink his ship in 1590. The advocates used sophisticated arguments to ridicule these charges calling them dreams and idle visions rather than a serious criminal charge. They stated that the indictment, and by implication the authorities in Eyemouth, had not even had the wit to dream up a storm raising like the North Berwick witches. The Edinburgh court would smirk at the stupidity of their country cousins down in the Borders. The advocates continued in the same vein, why not have Elizabeth and the other witches fly round the ship like crows. This was a clever move. There are very few instances of Scottish witches flying, it was a much more common occurrence on the continent. These lawyers were learned in both law and European tradition. Pandering to the intellect and egos of the Edinburgh courts they mocked the charges to great effect.

They then turned to some of the lesser offences managing to have the charges of making George Sprot poor and Margaret Homes' horse mad dropped from the dittay (legal charge). Probably as the cause and effect could not definitively be linked. After this brief interlude they moved onto more serious matters. The charge of conjuration and running widdershins was also thrown out. This was important as both actions were strong indicators of witchcraft with a diabolical element. The next two charges were of burying the horseshoe given to her by the Devil and of having been seen by two men talking to the Devil in her shift. Both of these charges were also thrown out. Her defence team then moved on to the two most serious charges that she had been delated by two known witches Margaret Ballanie and William Mearns. Somehow they managed to argue that these charges were not relevant and were dropped from the indictment against her. This was a major victory. To be delated by another witch was an almost certain death sentence. While the other charges still stood, including the two murder charges, if she had had no contact with the Devil and was not a witch as the Crown had originally stated then how and why would she murder?

The jury was of a similar mind. Elizabeth Bathgate was acquitted of all charges against her. The other witches were not so lucky. Patrick Smith was found dead in his cell in Eyemouth gaol. Worse was to come, somehow William Mearns had managed to escape from gaol and during the escape found enough rope to hang himself. It was said that he *'put hands on himself at the devill's instigation'*. Both bodies were committed to unhallowed ground. Tales were muttered about guards that left open doors and escaping prisoners that *'found'* rope. Margaret Ballanie, Alison Wilson, Agnes Wilson and Elspeth Wilson were all found guilty of witchcraft and legally worriet before their bodies were burnt.

So why was Elizabeth acquitted? Elizabeth Bathgate lodged four complaints before and during her trial. While this was not unknown it was generally dismissed unless there was gross illegality going on. In Elizabeth's case the complaints were upheld to the extent that Sir Patrick Hume was barred from giving evidence against her due to his *'gross prejudice'* against her. Sir Patrick may have been a knight of the realm but Elizabeth stood firm. While the prosecution team was led by the local aristocracy and numbered eleven prosecutors, investigators and expert witnesses Elizabeth, wife of a maltman, managed to afford to muster a defence team of four including three defence advocates so influential that they managed to have the trial transferred to Edinburgh where Elizabeth would not face a local jury that knew her. Was her defence team brilliant, was the prosecution team poor or was something else going on? Why was Sir Patrick so prejudiced against her? And why was she acquitted when the others were found guilty?

Sir Patrick's hatred of Elizabeth could have a number of reasons but for it so have been so strong as to warrant censure from the Privy Council it must have had a good cause, at least in Sir Patrick's mind. As a member of the local nobility he would have been extremely influential during the trial proceedings and this is probably why the defence team fought to have the trial moved to Edinburgh where his influence would be lessened. But this does not explain Elizabeth's acquittal. Was she about to name someone that was so powerful, even more so than Sir Patrick, that her acquittal was necessary to buy her silence and prevent a scandal? Or was it more ordinary than that?

Elizabeth's defence team persuaded the authorities to move the trial, they outlined Sir Patrick's malice towards Elizabeth, they detailed the fact that witness depositions had been taken outwith her presence, and not in a court of justice. They also managed to get some of these statements disallowed as the deponers had not come to Edinburgh to ratify them. During the actual trial they used legal arguments to defeat several of the charges against her. The advocates demanded the legal niceties were adhered to. In short, Elizabeth's team, did their job. The fact that the other accused witches, tried in Eyemouth, were found guilty merely adds to this. Had they had access to advocates they too might have been acquitted. The case against Elizabeth and her co-accused was quite simply not strong enough but in Eyemouth with Sir Patrick presiding convictions were a foregone conclusion.

The prosecution team consisted of:
    Sir Patrick Hume, with a complaint of false imprisonment
    against him upheld by the Privy Council
    George Hume, Minister of Aytoun, deprived of his ministry
    in 1650 after an unspecified complaint about his behaviour,
    complaint of false imprisonment against him upheld by the
    Privy Council
    John Hume, Minister of Eyemouth, complaint of false
    imprisonment against him upheld by the Privy Council
    Sir Thomas Hope of Craighall, Knight Baronet
    Sir Thomas Hope of Craighall, son of Sir Thomans Hope, Knight
    Baronet
    Issobel Kerr, wife of Sir Patrick and acting as expert witness
    Christopher Knowles, Minister at Coldingham, dismissed for
    adultery in 1641
    Sir John Ramsay of Edington
    Mark Hume
    John Oliphant
    Isobel Young

The 1634 case was a classic witchcraft trial in which the local nobility and Kirk conspired to convict eight people. Elizabeth Bathgate's trial was heard in Edinburgh with a defence team of three advocates. All of the other named witches were tried in Eyemouth without any defence. The advocates in Elizabeth's trial exposed the evidence for what it was, rumour and gossip. Rumour and gossip that had been presented by the local Kirk and nobility as evidence of guilt.

The evidence that convicted Margaret Ballanie, Alison Wilson, Agnes Wilson, Elspeth Wilson, Jennet Williamson and Patrick Smith was the same as the evidence that acquitted Elizabeth Bathgate. Elizabeth, due to her comparative wealth, was able to retain the services of advocates. It was that difference that saved her life.

No sentence was ever brought against Sir Patrick and the other for their false imprisonment of Elizabeth Bathgate.

That witches existed the Kirk had no doubt. All the most learned church men and philosophers of Western Europe had written numerous books on the subject. Even King James VI himself had written on the subject after the incident when the witches of North Berwick had raised a storm to try and drown him. The religious wars that had ravaged Europe in the wake of the Reformation had thrown the world into turmoil. While princes and emperors turned to the sword to protect their territories and root out heretics, church men and philosophers sought the path of learning to offer certainty and security in troubled times. Heretics lurked round every corner and the Devil, his witches and their wicked arts threatened faith and faithful alike. While the Reformation may have split mother church, learned manuscripts on witchcraft were eagerly sought by all no matter the faith of the author. All Christendom was in peril and the question was how to bring witches swiftly and securely to justice.

Between the mid 15th and mid 17th centuries several major manuscripts and treatises were written to help churchmen in their never ending battle against heretics and witches. While there were a few writers that disputed the existence of both witches and witchcraft they were overwhelmingly in the minority. The vast majority of manuscripts, taking the existence of witches as self evident, outlined in great detail how to identify and prosecute those witches. Written by theologians, lawyers and philosophers it was these manuscripts that laid the basis of the proofs acceptable to courts throughout Europe.

The Scottish courts recognised four proofs of an individual being a witch; having a history of bad behaviour, of evils acts, being named witch by another witch, confessing to being a witch and being found with the Devil's mark on the body. Arrest usually followed on from a direct accusation of having committed an act of witchcraft but was usually accompanied by a history of bad behaviour.

A bad reputation which could be built up over a number of years was a dangerous attribute to develop especially in a small community. This was more than just not being liked in an area, it was where an individual had a history of suspicious behaviour or of practising witchcraft. Many of those arrested had been performing witchcraft for many years often for friends or neighbours perhaps by helping find lost property and curing sickness with charms and chants. They may even have had a previous conviction for witchcraft. Occasionally a local Presbytery would, if someone was found guilty, merely excommunicate them from the Kirk or if the offence was relatively minor merely admonish them. However as the years went on the reputation might grow worse and instead of curing illness the individual might be suspected of causing illness.

The court records give sad testimony to this aspect of 'proof' and how mundane and easily it could be attained. Arguing with your neighbours or even your husband was always suspect and as much of life then was public, the market place, the farm, the town square, a family squabble could all too easily be seen and heard. Complaining about service or goods was also a minefield. An assertion that the butter you had bought had been spoiled could over time make your name as a 'quarrelsome' person.

And then there were the big two, non attendance at the Kirk and the death of a husband. Unless ill, and severely so, not going to the Kirk on Sunday was unthinkable. Human memory is an imperfect tool so that non attendance could be remembered and commented upon long after the cause of it was forgotten. Death of a spouse also raised suspicion. A man who lost his wife in childbirth was to be pitied while a woman who lost her husband due to natural causes was to be avoided.

Many trial records note a bad reputation going back over ten and even twenty years. Neighbours and Ministers who reported on the suspect were seldom questioned as to the veracity of their statements and local gossip became enshrined as proof once recorded by court clerks.

Of the trial records existing in Scotland 7% of those were below the age of twenty, 8% were between 20 and 30, 22% were between 30 and 40, 22% were between 40 and 50, and 38% were over 50. A history of 'witch' behaviour over many years would build up until a final or more severe charge was laid and an arrest made. Those under the age of twenty tended to be the sons, and more frequently, daughters of known witches.

There was also the aspect of changing attitudes. Being known as a witch in 1580 would bring the disapproval and condemnation of the Kirk, by 1600 the same, possibly trivial, offences were viewed more seriously and dealt with more harshly. So that previous arguments over crops or food which had been relatively innocent developed more sinister overtones. Stories of illnesses brought on after an argument or good fortune turning to bad would more readily be attributed to an act of witchcraft and taken by the courts as fact.

Another aspect of the heightened times and fears developed whereby a reputation could, unfortunately, be inherited. A mother, and in some cases a grandmother, who had previously had a reputation as a witch could result in a daughter being arrested. The logic being that had the daughter been a good Christian, she would have reported the mother as a witch. If no report was forthcoming then the daughter, or son, must be a witch as well. Several court records list mother and daughters as co-accused.

If a suspected or known witch named or 'delated' another individual this was considered strong proof of witchcraft. Those named by another witch rarely escaped a guilty verdict. Interrogations of suspected witches always included being asked about accomplices in the particular crime under investigation or of any other known witches. Interrogators would press hard on this point eager to round up all the guilty parties. Suspects would frequently be asked who had inducted them into witchcraft e.g. their mother or close relative, who had led them to dance with the Devil. It was common for a woman and her daughters to be arrested together and pressed to name each other as witches.

It was commonly believed that witches were inducted into a pact with the Devil when others were present and questioning would frequently follow this line of reasoning. A witch would be asked what other witches were present when they met the Devil. Witches were also thought to congregate, even if the Devil was not present, to carry out their witchcraft. Meetings with other women in the evening or at night, even if for no more sinister reason than to pass the time of day, would be suspect. Even where witches worked alone it was thought that one witch could recognise another and so pressure was brought to bear to name others.

The third proof of witchcraft and the one the interrogators aimed for was a formal confession of being a witch. This usually took the form of a confession of meeting the Devil either alone or in the company of other witches. The witch would then enter into a pact with the Devil and thus reject Christ. The form of the pact and how easily they had entered into it was important. The Kirk strove to prove the Devil as false and a liar and so the detail of what he had promised the witch and, hopefully, then failed to deliver was detailed not just to gain proof of witchcraft but also as an edification to other as to the true nature of the Devil.

The women frequently talked of having had sex with the Devil and again detail was sought. Descriptions of the Devil's nature were an important point for the Kirk. The Devil's penis was believed to be cold and this detail was given great prominence in the court evidence. The woman would then go on to list what deeds they had committed as a witch: the laying on of sickness or the ruining of food. In short they were expected to list grievances against themselves usually far exceeding the initial charges that had been laid.

Confession was always sought by the Kirk and those who did not confess were almost always assumed to be liars rather than innocent.

As the individual had probably already been named by another witch and had a reputation as a witch to deny it was deemed impudent arrogance. The suspect had been named and was a known witch how dare they refuse to confess when confronted by the Kirk with their own guilt. By not confessing the witch was challenging the authority of the local Kirk that had brought the charges against her. She was as good as calling the local Minister and Elders liars. She had to be made to confess to prove God's power. Kirk Elders would make it a point of pride to boast that they had brought their witches to confession, whilst those unable to do similar would keep quiet.

As the century wore on however, this zeal to bring witches to confession would lead to many of the excesses of torture and ill treatment. Ministers would not only look to nearby parishes for comparisons but also further afield and local pride became inflated when the large number of witches caught and brought to confession in the Borders was noted. The Devil always the attacked the most Godly, so the more witches caught and made to confess proved the Godliness of the Border's Presbyteries compared to other areas. A witch's confession to a compact with the Devil, perversely proved the Godliness of the community.

The fourth and final proof was the existence of the Devil's mark. One of the major points of debate amongst scholars of the time was whether or not witches could act without the Devil. This was a serious matter. Could witches, for the most part women, commit evil acts? To admit this was to afford them a power not natural to women. While the malice and evil that lurked in witches/women was not denied how this was harnessed by the Devil and ultimately allowed by God was a theological puzzle. In the Calvinist Kirk the understanding however was much clearer, witches were the handmaidens of the Devil and would be proved so to be.

It was believed that the Devil would mark his followers to seal their pact with him as a parody of Christian baptism. As in baptism the sign of the cross was made on the skin, so the Devil too would mark his followers. The mark was usually thought to be on the shoulder, although it could be anywhere on the body, where it was believed the Devil had laid his hand on the witch. This again parodied the laying on of hands by Christ. As the Devil was unnatural, it was believed that this mark would be insensitive to touch and would not bleed if pricked with a pin. The mark itself might be a visible blemish or merely a point on the body where no sensation was felt. This lack of sensation was seen as part of the Devil's trickery as he had tried to hide the evidence of the pact.

The Devil's mark was found by pricking the accused witch with a pin or bodkin. This was carried out either by the interrogators or more usually by professional witch-prickers specially brought in by the authorities. Pricking was usually carried out where a suspected witch refused to confess and could often result in both finding the Devil's mark and a confession. Pricking or 'brodding' as it was called was not considered torture but was merely part of the normal interrogation procedure. With these proofs in place the witch could be brought to trial.

5. STOW 1649

'ane great syckness'

itchcraft was not confined to the big border towns and in 1630 the village of Stow imposed a tax of £2 on each plough in the parish to maintain warded witches. In its day this was a large tax and on a village totally dependent of farming would have been a considerable burden to bear. So why was it imposed? Was Stow so full of witches that they cost so much to keep until trial, or were all the witches in Stow so poor that a tax had to be raised lest they starve to death before coming to trial? Possibly both factors came into play. There is no record however, of any complaints anent the tax perhaps indicating just how seriously the threat of witchcraft was taken. In such an agriculturally dependent area it was surely better to pay £2 towards the detection and prosecution of a witch than to have the harvest fail. Nineteen years later, in 1649, the tax was to be put to good use.

Stow village, sitting alongside the Gala water, was typical of Border villages of the time. Little more than a straggle of cottages and outlying farms, its inhabitants were for the most part poor with all that that entailed. Farming dominated the village with a mixture of sheep and kye. Although blessed with good water and grazing, this good fortune had seen many a Border Reiver come up the valley to take what they could steal from the defenceless village. They had suffered in 1648 as famine had struck the entire Borders and both people and animals had starved to death in that winter. The spring had been a welcome relief when suddenly kye were seen to sicken and die.

There could be only one explanation for these troubles and the word was out, witch. The name Isobel Thompson has been mentioned to the Minister and the investigation began. A young man from Lauder was also named and quickly brought to book. Brought before the Elders he quickly confessed and named Isobel as his accomplice. She had, he claimed, seduced the man over several nights and initiated him into witchcraft. Isobel was arrested and the two were locked up in the cellar of the Baillie's house. The Stow Elders' wrote to the Privy Council in Edinburgh for a Commission to try the two witches.

Isobel was in serious trouble, 'delated' as a witch by an accused witch was one of the four main proofs of witchcraft and more was to come. Unmarried, Isobel lived alone and did not appear to have had any support. But what she did have was a sharp tongue, an unfortunate inability to keep her temper and a reputation as a quarrelsome dame. There had been no hesitation or demur when her name was raised. By the time she was brought before the Elders her reputation had been examined and found wanting. Old arguments and half remembered disagreements had been discussed by the Elders. Ill repute was being added to being delated. More and more accusations were now coming in.

Unbowed by the wrath of the Minister and denying everything put to her, Isobel refused to confess. Hard questioning then turned to hard walking which went on long into the night and eventually a confession of sorts was extracted. Isobel had confessed to witchcraft but had also named another Margaret Dunholme. Margaret was also from Stow and also unmarried. She was soon arrested and joined Isobel and the Lauder man in the Baillie's cellar.

The formal Commission had been received from Edinburgh. With the permissions in place, the formal charges could now be laid. The final list of charges laid against the three were possibly as bad as they could be in a rural community, short of murder, and centred round the ruining of one local farmer by putting *'ane great syckness on his kye'*. Within the week his cattle had started to sicken and die and Isobel and the others were identified as the cause.

Unluckily for Isobel, Margaret and their male co-accused facing weeks incarcerated in an airless cellar awaiting trial, the summer was proving to be hot and sticky. And while statements had to be been taken and a jury found and sworn in, hands were needed in the fields. Who had time to sit in a courtroom? However, finally in the late summer the trial began.

The charges of witchcraft were formally laid, denial of God, using witchcraft to sicken and kill kye, using witchcraft to ruin crops. All three had, under questioning and walking, confessed and these confessions were read out. The denial of God and the turning to the Devil's ways was, in the eyes of the Kirk, the major crime. The Minister reminded all of the crisis that was facing the land as the Godless strove to overthrow the normal order. For a farming community, the more life threatening crime was the death of livestock. Coming so soon after a famine year, the death of kye could mean starvation for an entire family. A local jury delivered the verdict, guilty. The sentence, to be worriet and then burnt to death. The Kirk Elders congratulated each other. Three more of the Devil's followers would be consigned to the flames. The righteous had triumphed and all would see that evil was always found out. The village breathed a collective sigh of relief, life could get back to normal.

But the respite was brief. The ungodly were not finished with Stow yet. While the Kirk prepared for the execution of Isobel, Margaret and the Lauder man muttered suspicions were again heard in the village. The Elders may have been preparing to dispatch these three witches to hell fire but more witches were abroad that summer. Three names were muttered. The trial had fixed everyone's attention, but what of the rest of the happenings in the village? The muttering grew louder and the relief disappeared like a morning mist. James Henrison, Jonet Henrison and Marion Henrison were named - witches.

Reputations were once again under investigation. Vague suspicions were shared but while they could not be ignored, the three, although suspect, had not been delated and so further proof was needed. The Elders met and sat long into the night. What was to be done? Stow sent for John Kincaid.

In the meantime, the three Henrisons were arrested and locked in the Kirk. It was not thought fit to allow them to be locked in with the three convicted witches. Three in the Baillie's cellar, three in the Kirk, more men were needed to guard them. Men were needed for the building of the execution pyre but also for walking and watching. And a new jury would have to be sworn in once the new trial began. This time everyone would be called on to do their duty.

The next morning saw James, Jonet and Marion standing before the foremost witch pricker in Scotland. Word had spread round the village, Kincaid was here. A crowd gathered, three witches to be burnt, three more suspected, and the great John Kincaid in the village the murmurs grew. The Elders of the Kirk knew their flock and knew what could happen when fear gave way to panic, a firm hand was needed. They had met with Kincaid that morning and explained their predicament. This was a sore test for the Elders. Three more witches in tiny Stow. Well they would not be found wanting in their duty. They would root out the Devil and all his works. Kincaid listened carefully to their instructions. His experience in these matters was well known and his counsel to the Elders duly noted. They were decided, he was to be given a free rein.

James, Jonet and Marion stood before Kincaid flanked on either side by the Baillie's men. The Elders entered and the interrogation could begin. Questioned as to whether any of them were witches all three denied the charge. Kincaid put to work. James was stripped naked and shaved and made to stand before Kincaid. The pricker examined James' body for any blemish or spot that might be the Devil's mark. As James was held by the arms Kincaid brodded him in several places about the neck and shoulders. This involved pushing a two or three inch steel pin or bodkin into the persons body. The first few attempts drew blood but eventually a small insensitive spot that did not bleed was found. The Devil's mark was discovered. This was duly recorded and James was returned to the Kirk while Jonet was brought before Kincaid. Jonet was stripped and shaved and again brodded with the Bodkin until the Devil's mark was also found on her. The procedure was then repeated on Marion. Kincaid was paid six pounds Scots for the brodding, with a further three pounds paid by the Stow parish for meat and drink for Kincaid and his servant.

Jonet, Marion and James' trial began the next day. Witness statements had been taken and the jury sworn in. The charges against them centred on the discovery of the Devil's mark. All three were found guilty and sentenced to death.

Isobel, Margaret and the young Lauder man were taken out of the cellar led out to the edge of the Gala water and then worriet and burnt on the pyre. One week later Jonet, Marion and James followed them.

Plague

Plague was an all too common occurrence in the 17th century but with modern medicine it is hard to understand just how the word alone could instil such fear and panic in a population.

In 1349 the Scots and the English were once again indulging in their respective national pastimes of fighting each other in the Scottish Borders. The Scots fervently believed that God was on their side and this was proved when the English army started to sicken and die of an unknown and foul disease. This was surely God's punishment on the English for their wicked ways. Unfortunately the 'foul death of the English' was no respecter of geographical boundaries or nationality and within months the Scots army too was felled. As the Scots fled before the English and the pestilence sent by God they carried the disease to their homes and families throughout Scotland.

The Great Pestilence (the term the Black Death was invented around 1800) would devastate Europe killing around twenty million, about a third of the population at the time, and ruining and changing life for ever. It has been credited with ushering in the end of the feudal system and so marked society that the folk memory of the ensuing terror lingers on even to this day.

What struck terror into the hearts of communities was the speed of spread and the apparant indiscriminate manner in which some individuals lived while others died writhing in agony as the black buboes or swellings attacked the victims.

Two hundred and fifty years later was to see the start of a new century that was marked by outbreaks of plague - had the Great Pestilence returned?

Of the six outbreaks of plague that were seen in the Borders in the 17th century none were the Great Pestilence. Cholera or Typhoid are the most likely culprits. This was however no comfort to those in villages and towns when the cry went up - plague. What would it be this time, Cholera, Typhoid? Both resulted in death. Was it even the return of the Great Pestilence? London, that great city of sin and iniquity had seen the Great Pestilence return in 1666 where around 100,000 died.

Plague, in all its forms, was surely sent by God as a punishment for the sins of the wicked but, as had been seen in the Great Pestilence, had also inexplicably killed the Godly. With such an unknowable and deadly foe fear of the plague, in whatever form, was entirely justified and undertandable.

Witch hunting was a serious and Godly business and those involved did so for religious reasons. The uncovering and prosecution of witches was a duty in which everyone in a parish was expected to participate. However there were those possessed of a special skill in detecting witches and these were the witch prickers. There were around ten witch prickers in Scotland and these individuals, all men, would travel round the country, for a fee, aiding interrogations and giving evidence to Commissions.

In becoming a witch the woman or man had denied her baptism and the Devil had laid his mark on the witch. In making their compact with the Devil the deal would be sealed with the laying on of the Devil's hand. Parodying the Christian baptism, the mark was thought to be the visible sign of the invisible pact. Again the great theologians and philosophers took up their pens to write on the matter. Debate was engaged as to the size and location of marks, what was their level of sensation, whether they would draw blood if pricked and even whether or not every witch was marked by the Devil.

The Devil's mark was generally, though not always, found on the shoulder. It could also be found on the head or neck or, less commonly in Scotland, on other parts of the body. The witch's head would be shaved and then the shoulder, head and neck searched for the mark. If not found then the whole body would be shaved and searched. The mark itself might be anything, a small mole or freckle, a birthmark or a wart and could be large or small.

Pricking or 'brodding' a mark once it had been found involved inserting a long steel pin or bodkin into the flesh. These bodkins could be anything up to three inches long. Devil's marks were thought to be both insensitive to pain and unable to bleed as they had been caused by the unnatural Devil. Some thought the lack of sensitivity to be part of the Devil's attempts to hide the mark.

As the Devil's mark was so important, as one of the four proofs of witchcraft, and the Devil and witch would try their utmost to hide the mark, witch pricking was the preserve of experts. If a mark was not found on a suspected witch this was not taken as evidence of innocence but that the witch had somehow 'hidden' the mark. This was also true where a mark 'disappeared'. Suspected witches were often bodily searched by Baillies or Sherrifs before the arrival of an official witch pricker. The Baillie, having found a mark, would record the same. When searched by the witch pricker, if the mark was then found to be missing, this was taken as proof not of any error by Baillie or Sheriff but as part of the trickery of the witch in making the mark 'disappear'.

As in all aspects of human life where money is to be made the greedy, the venal and the plain charlatans are always to be found, witch pricking was no exception.

John Balfour plied his trade as a pricker in the early part of the century. In 1632, concerns were raised that he *goes athort the countrie abusing simple and ignorant people for his private gayne*. He was called before the Privy Council to answer these charges. The Council were not convinced as to his level of knowledge or expertise in the matter and he was forbidden from continuing to practise. Several questions remain unanswered. Why, prior to 1632, had he been able to work without any official warrant? Who had first recommended him to the Kirk? And when he was first employed by the Kirk why was no official warrant or authorisation sought? Although barred from working as a pricker, no charges appear to have been laid against him for the torture of suspects brodded by him.

In 1650, George Craithie was under suspicion. Having spent several years previously working as a pricker and no doubt earning a goodly sum, Craithie's own greed was to be his downfall. And this time it would be the Kirk who would catch him out.

Jonet Coutts had been arrested and confessed to witchcraft before the Haddington Presbytery in East Lothian. Jonet had, in her confession, named several other witches from East Lothian. Jonet however, was from Peebles and did not know Haddington well; she had named several local women of good character. Jonet was brought before the interrogators to explain herself and confessed that she had struck a bargain with Craithie. The deal was a simple one. She was to name as many witches as possible. He would then be *put to try anent the witches' mark and to profit thereby* and would then try to get Jonet's sentence reduced from execution to a lesser penalty. Craithie was called before the Kirk to answer the charges. He gave a firm denial of any bargain. The Kirk did not believe him and asked the civil authorities to deal with him. Although a request for arrest was made, no records remain as to whether or not this was carried out. Jonet was executed.

The use of witch pricking had another more sinister aspect. Authorised or not, the practise allowed those of a sadistic mind to ply their trade with the apparent blessing of the Kirk. One such appears to have been Jon Dick who, on more than one occasion, brodded suspected witches to death. Dick was arrested in 1662 and imprisoned in the Tolbooth in Edinburgh. Complaints had been raised that he had worked without the required authority, had shaved and humiliated prisoners and that in some cases prisoners had been *'pricked to death'*.

There is no doubt that an inexperienced pricker might cause the accidental death of a prisoner by blood loss or shock, this does not appear to have been the situation in this case however. Dick appears to have being accused of the death of more than one suspect. Privy Council records state that *'ane cheating fellow, named Jon Dick ...thereafter pricking him* (the suspected witch) *to the great effusion of his blood and with much torture to his body'*. Mr Dick was, it appears, a sadist. What appears to be of greater concern to the Privy Council however was the fact of him being *'ane cheating fellow'*. This challenge to their authority, by Dick overstepping the bounds in his treatment of prisoners, was their main concern. They would, it appears, have been equally outraged had he challenged their authority by ordering the release of a prisoner. The sadism was superfluous to the charge of challenging the authority of the state. Within this mindset, sadism could go on unchallenged.

The most famous witch pricker in Scotland was undoubtedly John Kincaid from East Lothian. Kincaid was from Tranent and became famous throughout Scotland for his uncanny ability to find the Devil's mark on any witch no matter how cunningly hidden. Working between 1649 and 1662 it is not known how many witches were sent to the flames as a result of Kincaid's work but the figure must be in excess of two hundred.

In his time Kincaid travelled between Edinburgh and the Lothians and as far north as Stirling and as far west as Glasgow but he was frequently to be found in Border towns. Called in by the Kirk to help in the cases of uncooperative suspects he travelled to towns and villages alike and would come as ready to brod twenty as one. His name is repeated time and time again in trial records right through the 1650s with the apparent blessing of the Privy Council. He, presumably, was working with the requisite legal authority.

In 1662 however, accusations were raised against Kincaid and a warrant was issued for his arrest by the Privy Council. Two main charges were levelled at Kincaid: that he had wrongly found the Devil's mark on innocent victims and, more importantly, that he had been brodding suspects without having a warrant to do so. Kincaid, it seems, had succumbed like others to the witch hunting fever and had acted without due process of the law. The official report submitted to the Privy Council stated that Kincaid had worked '*without warrand and order to prick and try these persons*'. More damning was the statement that '*there hath bein great abuses committed by John Kincaid*', concluding that '*in all probabilitie many innocents have suffered*'. The numbers are not stated but records show several appeals by individuals pleading for release on the grounds that they had been unlawfully brodded and that other than the mark found by Kincaid there was no evidence against them. The Privy Council had to act. Kincaid was arrested and sent to the Tolbooth in Edinburgh.

It is not known when and why Kincaid started working without the necessary warrants that he had, presumably, previously always sought and obtained. Was it for personal reason? Or was this under pressure from Kirk Ministers in far flung rural parishes anxious to consign a witch to the flames quickly and without waiting for the paperwork to be completed?

After some two months in gaol Kincaid petitioned the Privy Council for his release. This was granted, after he had posted bail of £1,000 Scots and agreed that he would no longer work as a witch finder without the correct warrant. The Privy Council was concerned that Kincaid, who was by now an old infirm man, would die in gaol. The Council did not ban him from working as a witch pricker but merely wanted the assurance that he would always obtain a warrant to do so in the future. There is no record of any further action taken against Kincaid. The situation of the '*many innocents (that) have suffered*' was forgotten.

The £1,000 Scots Kincaid posted as surety was an extremely large sum of money which may in part answer why he had worked without warrants. To be able to raise £1,000 in a two month period hints that Kincaid was, by this time in his life, relatively wealthy. It may well be that part, if not all, of that wealth had been generated by witch hunting. The temptation to work quickly and without a warrant for money had proved a great temptation for other prickers, it may well be that Kincaid too fell victim to such a temptation.

Witch prickers were one of the few individuals involved in witchcraft trials that made a living. As they were paid for every witch they detected it was in their own interests to find more witches. While some, no doubt, thought they were doing God's work many others saw an opportunity to make money and a few to indulge in sadistic acts for their own pleasure. And for those who were carrying out God's work? At the hands of these men, and they were all men, some victims were brodded to death, while many more suffered extreme humiliation and pain. Almost all were then executed.

Although brodding fell into disuse in the latter half of the century as the many abuses came to light, it remained, for many in the Kirk as well as the Privy Council, the preferred method for finding out the Devil's own. The problem was not felt to be with brodding but with those who professed to have the skill yet did not and, more importantly, those who claimed the authority to work as witch prickers without any warrant from the Privy Council. Brodding was discouraged as abuses called the authority of the Privy Council into question. Had a more robust system of authorisation and monitoring of witch prickers being developed, the search for the Devil's mark with steel bodkins would, no doubt, have continued.

However, what was officially discouraged continued in practise in many rural areas for some years to come. Unofficial, self appointed witch hunters would, for a reasonable fee, help local parishes in the discovery of witches and in bringing them to confession through the discovery of their Devil's mark. Cases of brodding, which could be carried out over several weeks until a mark was found, were recorded as late as 1684 in the Borders.

6. LAUDER 1649

'the devil is a lyer'

cross the moor from Stow the guid folk of Lauder had watched and listened in horror at the events taking place in their small neighbour, ever thankful that the Lord had spared them. But as the year drew on rumours grew that Lauder was not to be spared from the Devil and his ilk. Hob Grieve had lived in Lauder all his life and, although known throughout the town as a man who had married a witch, was thought no more than a harmless fool. His wife had been executed well over twenty years previously, a deserving shrew by local accounts, and Hob had managed a living by working here and there on odd jobs. One of the poorer inhabitants of the town he was nonetheless a cheery fellow that liked an ale of a summer evening.

That however was the problem. One evening sitting with some local worthies talking of the troubles in Stow Hob had let slip how his wife had taken him to meet a great gentleman at the Gala water just a little south of Stow. No more was said but a few glances were exchanged. Within the week the Minister came to call on Hob and after some close questioning Mr Byres saddled his horse and rode across the moor to speak to Mr Cleland at Stow.

Thomas Byres and John Cleland invited a third Minister, John Veitch from Bassendean, to join them in their deliberations. John Veitch was known as a hard man that had refused to conform to Episcopacy and in 1662 would be deprived of his parish. He was outlawed in 1680 and imprisoned in 1683. He returned to his parish in 1690 and, until his death in 1692, dogmatically stuck to his belief in the inherent evil that was witchcraft. He continued to call for and deliver the sternest punishment possible for all convicted witches.

The three Ministers contemplated the case and after a night deep in thought wrote to the Privy Council for a Commission to investigate and try Hob Grieve and any others he might delate as witches. John Veitch offered his services as an investigator into the case. William and Gilbert Lauder the Baillies were instructed to bring Hob Grieve in for interrogation.

Hob was brought to the town's Tolbooth to await the visit from the Ministers. Armed with their bibles the three Ministers had Hob brought before them. Asked if he knew why he had been brought before them he answered simply *'forbye my wife was a witch'*. Prepared for a long and hard interrogation, the Ministers were quite unprepared for what Hob said next.

Hob told them that in 1629, he had been walking with his wife down at the Gala water near Stow. His wife, as always, was nagging him about his ways and said that she knew of a gentleman that would give him some good work and would help them get rich if they would but listen to him and do as they were bid. Hob then stated he saw a large mastiff dog the like of which he had never seen before and which amazed him. Just as soon as he had seen the dog it disappeared and a fine black man stood in his place. The gentlemen said if Hob would become but an officer in his service, attend meetings on the Sabbath and hold the door for all to come in he would be rich. Then Hob's tone changed and he sounded aggrieved as he told the Ministers that the Devil had deceived Hob who had remained poor all his days. When they came for his wife as a witch it was true that the Devil had protected him but Hob had never become rich and had thus taken a *'richt scunnert wi him'*.

But there was more to come. Hob then proceeded to tell the Ministers of all the people he had seen at the meetings, the names tumbled out of him in his eagerness to please. Isobel Brotherstane, Margaret Dalgleish, Janet Lyes, and Christian Smith. Hob stopped talking and was taken away to spend the night in the cells while the Ministers deliberated on what had occurred. The next morning Isobel Brotherstane came to the Tolbooth and, calling Hob a warlock, demanded to speak to him. William Lauder told her to go home but she refused. Eventually Hob was brought up from the cells.

Isobel challenged him, ' *thou common thief, how dare thou for they soul say that ever before this time thou say me or I saw thee, or ever was in thy company, either alone or with others?'*.

Hob turned to the Baillie, '*How come she then to know that I called her a witch?* Then facing Isobel asked, *Surely none but the Devil, they old master and mine, has told thee so much?* '.

Isobel replied, '*the Devil and thou perish together, for he is not my master though he be thine. I defy the Devil and all his works'*.

Hob then reminded her of all the times and places they had met while in the Devil's service.

Then Isobel replied again, '*Now I perceive that the Devil is a lyar and a murderer from the beginning, for this night he came to me, and told me to come and abuse thee; and never come away till I was confronted with thee, and he assured me that thou would deny all and say, thou false tongue, thou lyest.'*.

Brought before the Ministers Isobel then confessed to witchcraft and delated the same names as Hob but then added Issobel Raich. This last name caused some concern to Thomas Byres. Issobel Raich was known as a god fearing woman and he hesitated for a moment before taking down her name.

When Margaret Dalgleish, Janet Lyes, and Christian Smith were brought in they all confessed that yes they had denied their baptism that they had gone into the service of the black gentleman but that he had deceived them and they were all still very poor. All three of the women were in their forties and widows with no close family. They were amongst the poorest of the women in Lauder being practically destitute with no prospects of any improvment in their lives. They may have attended meetings with Hob deluding themselves that the Devil had indeed promised them a better life or they may have confessed after the usual treatment in the Tolbooth the records do not exist to give any more detail.

Issobel Raich was slightly younger than the rest being in her early thirties. A married woman with children and a working huband she was not poor by the standards of the day. Able to afford to have food and clothing brought into the Tolbooth she also did not suffer as much as her fellow prisoners. It does appear, however, that her husband abandoned her soon after her imprisonment. It is not clear who supplied her little luxuries although suspicion was to fall on one of the Magistrates.

The trial date was set for 2 October and Thomas Cranston, Edzer Young of Wedderlie, Robert Hart of St John's chapel and Alexander Hume sat as Magistrates.

So the six accused sat in Lauder Tolbooth to wait for the trial. It was assumed that Hob had been their leader and as such was kept apart from the others. Stories started to circulate about his powers and the Baillie and his men spent as little time as possible with their fearsome prisoner. Left to himself, confined to a cramped airless cell over the hot summer months Hob lost what little wits he had originally had and slowly went mad.

The trial was a subdued affair with the women repeating their confessions and little said. Everyone was waiting for Hob. Brought into court he was a dreadful sight. His hair lay long and unkempt down his back matched by his beard. Muttering to himself under his breath, curses and spells some would say, he appeared to disregard the Magistrates when questioned. John Veitch stepped up and read out his previous confession as a servant of the Devil. Hob laughed and said that he didn't care much for the Devil any more. He said that the Devil had once tried to drown him at Musselburgh when he had been carrying a heavy creel upon his back. Hob then said that he had a secret to tell but would tell only Mr Veitch. Shuffling up to the Minister Hob said that the Devil had come to him several times while he lay in the prison and threatened to cast him into the fire. Hob told the Minister that he didn't care and wasn't sacred as he was more powerful than the Devil now and could defeat him.

It took the Magistrates only one day to find Hob Grieve, Isobel Brotherstane, Margaret Dalgleish, Janet Lyes, and Christian Smith guilty of witchcraft. They were all sentenced to be worriet and then burnt. Mad Hob might have been but he was still to face the flames.

Issobel Raich had sat quietly and a little apart from the others during the trial and when her confession was read out, there was debate as to whether or not it was indeed a true confession or perhaps a story uttered by the fears of a frivolous women. Mention was also made of her previous good character but these considerations were severely brushed aside by John Veitch. Delated by a confessed witch her guilt was obvious. She too was sentenced to death.

On the day of her execution Issobel Raich spoke to the crowd.
'Now all you that see me this day, know that I am to die a witch by my own confession; and I free all men, especially the Ministers and Magistrate, of the guilt of my blood. I take it wholly on myself. My blood be upon my own head; and as I must make answer to the God of heaven presently, I declare I am as free of witchcraft as any child; but being delated by a malicious women, and put in prison under the name of a witch, disowned by my husband and friends, and seeing no ground of hope of my coming out of prison or ever coming in credit again, through a temptation of the Devil, I made up that confession on purpose to destroy my own life, being weary of it, and choosing rather to die than to live.'.

It was said that the '*temptation of the Devil*' had been an affair that Isobel was rumoured to have had with a member of the local nobility. Alexander Hume, one of the Presiding Magistrates, was suspected of helping Issobel with food and clothing while in the gaol. He had tried to have her confession disallowed and had sought her release. This was blocked by John Veitch.

Hob Grieve, Joke the Graham, there are few men named in the records but they are there. The most infamous was Dr Fian leader of the North Berwick witches who had tried to drown the King. Scotland, however, like most European countries saw witchcraft in terms of a female crime. Weak, lustful and easily corrupted it was little wonder that they became the Devil's wanton followers, but what about the men? What was their rôle and how did they fare in the courts?

Around 16% of those tried in Scotland as witches were men: while the figure in the Borders was lower around 8% or some 28 of those in the existing records.

Warlocks posed a problem for both the courts and the Kirk. Men, by their very nature, were steadfast and true in their faith, unlike women, and unlikely therefore to make a pact with the Devil. And if part of that pact had involved intercourse with the Devil, taking advantage of the lustful nature of women, where did that leave warlocks? Not even the most zealous of Kirk men suggested homosexual relations. Most crimes involved the laying on of sickness or ruining crops and ale; the concerns of women not the crimes of men.

Warlocks were men and as men were engaged in crimes more worthy of them. Raising bad weather was typical of this either to ground ships off the Berwickshire coast or to close the drove roads across the moors. Witches might be single women at the bottom of the pile as far as earnings and respect went but most warlocks were men of middling status, not individuals at the edges of communities. Farmers, small merchants and artisans with a certain standing in many towns and villages. Their crimes were often aimed at those with similar businesses. The failure of a fellow trader would be to their advantage or revenge could be sought where a previous business transaction had resulted in a loss of money or respect.

Warlocks were also to be found in leadership over several female witches. If the crimes were of a more lowly nature, curdling milk, laying of sickness on a pig, the natural order was restored by the directions for such crimes being given by a warlock while the work was carried out by witches. Warlocks may also have acted as an intermediary between the Devil and the witches. This was a further terrifying development. As Catholic priests interceded between God and ordinary people, did Warlocks fulfill the same purpose with the Devil? This was theologically dangerous territory. And could, potentially, give warlocks more diabolically bestowed powers.

But as men these were not passive female defendants, although plenty women proved to be pretty formidable. These were men that would resist arrest, demand a legal defence, cross examine witnesses and turn cases on their heads as they voiced counteraccusations and argument. A witch delated by a warlock would face the flames every time. A warlock accused by a witch could, by force of personality and using the accepted norms of the day, not only walk free but lay charges against the local Sheriff and Kirk Minister for false arrest and imprisonment. These were not men to be trifled with. The very nature of women laid them open to charges of witchcraft while their status in society weighed against them in the courts. For men the very opposite was true. Seldom suspected, when delated it was often dismissed as the spite and deceit of women. In some cases witches who delated a man of good standing had the accusation of malice added to the list of their diabolical crimes.

Even when arrested many warlocks were given bail and allowed to wait their time until trial at home. The courts, filled with male lawyers, prosecutors and juries, did not want to believe fellow men guilty and when the accused put up a robust defence, not guilty and not proven verdicts were frequently returned. Those who were found guilty were often old or poor or had lost their wits and even then could sometimes escape the flames merely to be flogged and excommunicated.

A comforting thought might have been that every warlock was addled in his wits. But while Hob Grieve may well have become mad as his treatment and incarceration had continued, there are no records to suggest that only the feeble minded were arrested and charged with being a warlock. The problem for the Kirk was in the very name, warlock. A witch was a woman who had denied God and given her self to the Devil; a warlock was an oath breaker. The Kirk demanded that men take responsibility for their belief: they were expected to pledge a solemn oath and covenant with God. A warlock, by taking up with the Devil, had made a conscious decision to break that oath. Time and again the bible exhorted the faithful to keep their oath to God. To become a warlock was to break that oath. In the eyes of the Kirk, there was no greater crime a man could commit.

There were of course certain men who, in the eyes of many, were already warlocks in all but name, Catholics. The heresy of the Catholic faith was anathema to the Kirk, a grey area for the courts and a political minefield for all. As Catholics they were denying the true faith but were, frustratingly, not under its jurisdiction. The wars of the Covenanters had won and the country was indeed a Protestant one but in pockets here and there the Catholics remained. Although very much in the minority in the Borders memories were long and Francis Stewart, Earl of Bothwell's involvement in the witchcraft case of North Berwick had not been forgotten. Acquitted of all charges against him, no doubt by diabolical means, he had later revealed his true nature by rejecting the true faith and becoming a Catholic. As an illegitimate son of James V and a member of the nobility, he was a terrifying example to the Kirk of the diabolical nature of Catholics.

There was also one type of warlock feared above all others and that was the Minister who was also a warlock. Diabolical Catholics may have evoked hatred in the Kirk but members of the Kirk themselves who broke their oath to God was surely a sign of the apocalypse. The Borders was, in this respect at least, spared that particular horror.

The majority of warlocks tried in the Borders were related to witches and as relatives would naturally have come under suspicion. The familiar tale of mundane sickness in children and kye was told and the Kirk interrogated and prosecuted. The theological drama of oath breaking sat side by side with accusations of charms and spells. While the records show a lower rate of both conviction and execution for warlocks than for witches, there is a higher rate of suicide. Was the loss of status and respect too great for these men to bear? Had they further to fall than their female colleagues and wished to spare their families more distress? Even though the conviction rate was lower for men than for women it was still higher than in most other crimes. A suicide in the family might have seemed better than a convicted warlock.

Or was it that, as men, they had greater access than women to the means by which to end their lives? Suicides by female suspects were not unknown but were rare. Often bound over in their own homes until the trial male suspects had ample means and opportunity to kill themselves. For those that were incarcerated, money would, no doubt, buy a stout rope and an hour of time when the guard would be conveniently elsewhere. As poorer members of the community such opportunities were denied their female counterparts. Of the recorded suicides in the Borders 67% were male, 22% were female with the remaining 11% of unknown gender.

Belief in witchcraft

Belief in witchcraft is often denigrated as a peculiarity of our superstitious and ignorant ancestors. So why in the 21st century do we still believe:

- *a black cat crossing your path is unlucky - a black cat was a witch's familiar (a creature thought to share the witch's supernatural power)*

- *a four leaf clover is lucky*

- *throwing a penny down a wishing well is lucky*

- *spilt salt should be thrown over the left shoulder to prevent bad luck - the salt will stop the Devil seeing you*

- *walking under a ladder is unlucky*

- *a horseshoe brings good luck - but must be the right way up or the Devil will pull the luck out*

- *seeing one magpie is unlucky*

- *touching wood brings good luck - the cross was made of wood and repels the Devil*

- *the empty shell from a boiled egg should always be pierced to let the Devil out*

- *a ring with a pearl will bring tears*

- *its unlucky for a groom to see the bride on the morning of the wedding before the ceremony*

- *the groom must carry the bride over the threshold -to stop the Devil nipping at her ankles*

- *the number thirteen is unlucky*

7. KELSO 1662

'pilliewinkles upon her fingers…
a grevious torture'

he spring of 1662 was a mild one. Famine had not been seen for over fourteen years and while not exactly a distant memory, neither was it a constant spectre to the villagers of Kelso. Lying on the banks of the Tweed Kelso was, in 1662, a remarkably quiet village. Barely ten miles from the border with England it had seen armies come and go in the past and would do so again but as the spring turned to summer it was no enemy army that would trouble the village but an ordinary woman, two children, an old woman and a Covenanter.

On 12 June Sir Archibald Douglas obtained a Commission from the Privy Council to try four confessed witches: Bessie Thomson, Malie Jonstoun, Agnes Quarie and Malie Turnbull. The Commission stated that Sir Douglas was to judge the four women and if found guilty, without the application of torture or other indirect means to extract confession, *'then and in these cases the saids commissioners (to) cause the sentence of death to be execute upon them and no otherways'*. The Commission was similar to hundreds of others that had been sought and issued throughout the century to various towns in the Borders with two crucial differences.

This Commission appeared, on the face of it, to prohibit the Commissioners from using torture or other indirect means to extract confession. Torture was routinely used and an acceptable practise until around 1661 and even thereafter its use was allowed as long as the correct permissions were sought. Indirect means such as sleep deprivation and walking were not considered torture but again were an accepted method by which to bring witches to confession and for which no permission was required. Why therefore, should the Privy Council wish to stop the use of torture in this case and why should they specify this within the Commission document itself?

The second difference was found in a later paragraph where the Commission states that the accused had to be both mentally and legally competent before any confession could be accepted. Children and those considered mentally incompetent had been known to stand trial previously. Why then should the Privy Council have specified, in this case, that those standing trial had to be sane and above the legal age of responsibility? Why was the Privy Council so concerned about legal procedures in Kelso?

Sir Archibald Douglas was a fervant Covenanter and was extremely outspoken in his condemnation of, as he saw it, any form of religious belief that was not strictly Presbyterian. Unfortunately for any accused witches brought before him this meant that interrogations carried out under Sir Archibald's jurisdiction were extreme in nature and all encompassing in their application. Being addled in your wits or under the age of sixteen was no protection from Sir Archibald's questioning. As the Privy Council had raised the issue of age it may be either that some of the four accused were below the age of sixteen, or that Sir Archibald had, on previous occasions, put children to torture.

Bessie Thomson, Malie Jonstoun, Agnes Quarie and Malie Turnbull had all confessed to some degree of witchcraft although the exact details are not known. Arrested by Sir Archibald, they were imprisoned and immediately interrogated. Whatever wickedness they confessed, it was enough for Sir Archibald and he applied to the Privy Council for a Commission. But the Privy Council asked for more details. And it was at that point that they laid the stipulations about torture, age and mental competency. The more detailed confessions, as demanded by the Privy Council, were to be obtained without torture and legal age and competence were to be ascertained and certified. The implication is clear enough Bessie, Malie, Agnes and Malie's first partial confessions to Sir Archibald had been obtained under torture. There is also some evidence to suggest that at least some of the accused were either children or mentally incompetent.

The Privy Council stated that they wished to see recorded the details of how the accused had renounced their baptism and had made a pact with the Devil. The Council wanted details of the pact, how had it been made, what had been said, what had been signed. The Kirk was exacting in its interrogation in these matters. This was, after all, the dark heart of the whole matter. However, these were details that only a competent adult could provide. The Privy Council, it seemed, knew Sir Archibald only too well. Without recourse to torture and with only children and those mentally impaired to question, the case fell. This is not to suppose the Privy Council of being concerned about the four accused no matter how young or senile. Rather they wished correct legal process to be followed and possibly, at the same time, to temper Sir Archibald and his local power.

While the Privy Council were attempting to curb the Covenanting excesses of Sir Archibald, from the safety of their Edinburgh chambers of course, the reality for the accused witches was somewhat different. The ages of the accused is not recorded but both Bessie Thomson and Malie Jonstoun would be in trouble with the authorities some twenty years later when they were described as being women in their late twenties or early thirties. This would seem to suggest that in 1662, when they were tortured by Sir Archibald, they could have been as young as eight or nine. Agnes Quarie would also be questioned in later years when she would be dismissed as an old women too fond of 'seeing the faeries'.

While all four accused were not executed they had suffered illegal imprisonment, interrogation and torture. They would have suffered, at the very least, sleep deprivation, psychological bullying, and of having been walked for hours on end. They might have been burnt with hot stones, had their skin rasped off with ropes or their fingers broken and crushed. All of this as well as being imprisoned for weeks away from their families and friends. Sir Archibald may have been thwarted in his zeal in pursuing this particular case but no records exist of any charges brought against him for his initial and illegal ill treatment of Bessie, Malie, Agnes and Malie.

While the existence of witches was, to the Kirk, self evident proof had to be brought before the Courts. The Witchcraft Act of 1563 stated,

'forsamekeill as the Quenis Maiestie and thre Estatis in this present Parliament being informit that the havy, abominabill superstitioun usit be divers of the liegis of this Realme be using of Witchcraftis, Sorsarie, and Necromancie, and credence gevin thairto in tymes bygane aganis the Law of God: and for avoyding and away putting of all sic vane superstitioun in tymes tocum; It is statute and ordanit be the Quenis Maiestie and thre Estatis forsaidis that na maner of persoun nor persounis of quhatsumever estate, degre, or conditioun thay be of tak upone hand in ony tymes heirefter to use ony maner of Wichcraftis, Sorsarie, or Necromancie: nor gif thame selfis furth to have ony sic craft or knawlege thairof, thairthrow abusand the pepill; Nor that na persoun seik ony help, response, or consultatioun at ony sic usaris(or abusaris) forisaidis of Wichcraftis, Sorsarie, and Necromancie, under the pane of dead: asweill to be execute aganis the user-abusar, as the seiker of the response or consultatioun. And this to be put to execution be the Justice Schireffis, Stewartis, Baillies, Lordis of Regaliteis and Rialteis, thair Deputis, and uthers Ordinar Jugeis competent within this Realme with all rigour, having powar to execute the samin.' .

The Act was clear, the interrogation of witches was to be executed *'with all vigour'*. Witches had to be made to confess by whatever means necessary. If proof was needed then interrogation would produce that proof. They had to be made to name any other witches involved and also what they had done in their dealings with the Devil and in their evil acts. And of course the Devil's mark had to be found on their body. But they were witches and had magical powers, why did they not escape from prison and from their treatment? They had in fact been abandoned. The Devil, who had promised them everything, was a liar and deceiver and this was proved by the fact that he had abandoned them to their fate. He has deserted them to face the torments of their treatment alone. This was the reasoning that lay behind the torture of witches.

Torture was freely allowed up to 1661 and if it was to be used thereafter permission had to be sought. It was rarely refused. However, permission often entailed sending a rider with a dispatch off to Edinburgh awaiting a reply, which could take several days to appear. As witch hunts and the attendant hysteria mounted local courts carried out interrogations with whatever methods they felt necessary often dispensing with their duty to seek the permission of the Privy Council. Speed was of the essence in the fight against the Devil and his hordes and zealous Kirk Elders applied torture safe in the knowledge of their own righteousness and confident in the guilt of the accused even if the necessary permission has not been sought or had not yet arrived. In cases where permission has been given local justice could often go far beyond what was legally allowed. This was a battle for the very souls of men and a little extra rough treatment here and there was preferable to allowing the Devil and his followers to overrun the earth.

Records indicate that torture, whether legally sanctioned or not, was commonly used in the Borders as late at 1690.

Types of torture included the Pilliewinkles. These were long metal boards that fitted over the fingers and were then screwed tighter and tighter. The fingers were crushed, the bones broken and the fingernails dragged out by the roots. They were so painful almost all victims became unconscious when they were applied and some were said to die from shock.

Ropes were also commonly used. A length of rope would be wound round the victim's foreheard and then twisted tight to apply pressure. This would twist and burn the skin and hair would often be wrenched out by the roots. Blood vessels, especially those in the eyes and nose, would rupture and bleed profusely and the one or both ear drums could be perforated. An account from the *News from Scotland* of 1591 lists the treatment of one witch '*the pilliewinkles upon her fingers, which is a grevious torture, and binding and wrenching her head with a cord or rope, which is a most cruel torture... and then she confessed all.*'.

Suspects could be burnt with hot stones. The local blacksmith would be called in the help in this matter, his expertise with fire integral to the procedure. The stones were heated in a pit and then spread in front of the victim who, barefoot, was made to stand on top of them. Victims who struggled too much or were unable to stand due to fatigue or previous ill treatment had the stones held against the soles of their feet.

The boot was another favoured method of extracting information. This comprised a large wooden boot that had holes in it through which further wooden pegs could be driven. The pegs could tear muscles, tendon, and ligaments and break bones in the foot and lower leg. The excrutiating pain was not the only consideration. Like the pilliewinkles, the boot could render a victim a cripple for the rest of their lives unable to earn a livelihood and under threat of starvation.

Hairshirts or hairshifts. These were made out of very coarse material similar to sacking and could, in some instances, shear a victim's skin off. More generally the skin would become raw with bleeding and extremely painful. The accused witch was forced to wear this for days on end. Most then developed skin infection from the dirt and exrement that were also around in the cells. Even when not forced to wear a hairshirt suspects often had no other clothing with which to cover themselves in winter.

Sleep deprivation and walking was also carried out. These were not classed as torture and so could be applied at will. Sleep deprivation is a very effective way of obtaining confessions, because it quickly leads to hallucination. It was usually undertaken by local authorities such as Burgh Bailies, or more frequently by the Kirk Elders. Quite simply accused witches were kept sitting on small stools and not allowed to put their feet on the ground for hours on end or told to stand up in a cell and not allowed to sit or lie down sometimes for two or more days.

Walking was equally brutal and again was carried out under the supervision of the Kirk Elders. Two men would take the suspect under each arm and walk her up and down her cell for around two hours. The two men would then be relieved by two fresh walkers. This could be continued for anything up to forty eight hours at a stretch. By the end of this time the prisoner would be exhausted, their feet and lower legs would be a pulpy and bloody mess. The blood loss and shock could result in death from dehydration and hypovoleamic shock. If the individual did not die - and the Balllies knew eactly when to stop, they would however have neuralgic pain on both legs which would be exacerbated afterwards by the lightest touch so that Baillies only had to tap the leg for it to send excrutiating pain up the legs to the small of the back.

Swiming witches was seldom used in Scotland, although it was used in a case in 1597. The records are scare for that time but it appears to have been discredited in some way and was not used thereafter. It was a test to see whether or not the suspect floated. The belief being that the water would rejected them as they had obviosuly rejected the baptism of Christ. The suspect was tied with ropes in such a way as to allow them to float but also to prevent them drowning. It was however a test that was open to abuse with many being drowned as a result of poor technique or perhaps deliberate malice. That may have been the reason why it was not used after 1597.

During all of these practices the suspects would be being constantly berated by the local Kirk Minister and Elders. Harangued and bullied they would be told that they were evil and wicked and would go straight to hell for all eternity for their crimes. Told how they were a disgrace and a source of shame and loathing to their families. Everybody hated and feared them, their filthy practices were known, their heresies had been exposed. Castigated as the Devil's whores and followers they were ridiculed and humiliated. This psychological abuse was heaped on them continously in a tirade of anger and disgust. Those who refused to co-operate could also be threatened that their families would be arrested and also tortured. This was often used where a suspect had a teenage daughter or son.

Their treatment in gaol was also harsh. While prison conditions were hard for all prisoners at that time they were particularly brutal for suspected witches. All prisoners had to pay for their own food and bedding and would sell anything they had to prevent starvation. However, many had nothing to sell. Many prisoners had basic food and bedding supplied by the local Kirk. This largesse was not, however, extended to suspected witches. The greatest effect on their treatment was their crime. The stigma of a charge of witchcraft was often enough to drive away any friends and family that could help. They would often exist on basic water and gruel, with little clothes and bedding. Cases of witchcraft could take several weeks to come to trial and their trials could last several more weeks so that victims were often close to starving by the end of their ordeal. Visits from friends and family, brave enough to want to visit, were often denied in case they brought any help. More often that not however, family would not visit for fear of being branded witch themselves.

While the Kirk was involved in witch cases at every level and supervised torture sessions they did not take any responsibility for the welfare of the suspects. The Kirk did however, pay the wages of prickers and warders. The plight of suspected witches was noted with cases recorded where suspected accused were reduced to '*drinking their own piss*' There are also several instances of Sheriffs complaining about half naked prisoners appearing before them in rags. The complaint being that their stench offended the noses of the authorities, not that the suspects had been starved.

Alongside *'official'* torture there were also many cases where suspects were simply beaten until they confessed. While there are very few records of complaints against beatings by Kirk Ministers, they do exist. What has been recorded however, in the costings of the interrogation, is the bill for two stout Kirk men to *'compel said prisoner'* On another occasion the cost of a new staff for the Minister is listed. Beatings were illegal, but usually accepted as necessary and the suspects own fault for showing such intransigence in refusing to confess. Any sympathy shown was for those Ministers who had to deal with such foul creatures.

It is true that the treatment of any prisoner in the 17th century was far from perfect and ill treatment and torture could and frequently was used in many instances. However, witchcraft appears to be the only crime where ill treatment was ordered, supervised and in some instances carried out by Kirk Ministers. The records also seem to indicate that far from being used as a means of last resort, as in most other crimes, torture or ill treatment of one kind or another was automatically used from the moment of arrest in the case of witchcraft. It is also the only crime in which age, gender and infirmity did not appear stay the hand or lessen the ill treatment.

Witches and Healers

Contrary to the popular misconception very few witches were actually midwives or healers. In the Scottish records that exist for the occupations of accused witches only around 4% were either midwives or healers. While this number would, not doubt, be greater were the records more complete, it is unlikely to result in the vast majority of suspects actually working as midwives or healers.

The reason for this is quite simple, the beliefs around illness and healing in the 17th century were intimately bound up in beliefs in witchcraft but in a negative rather than a positive sense. Illness could result from many sources once of which was, of course, from witches but in approaching another witch the individual suffering the illness wanted the spell, that is the original cause of the illness, removed. Once the spell was gone the illness would follow. So witches were more likely to be thought of as the cause of illness rather than as healers.

Medicine in the 17th century was divided between doctors, who treated the wealthy, and local home remedies that would be applied, in most instances, by the mother in the home. Where the cross over with witches occurred was when women sought advice from their own older sisters, or mothers, or other female relatives.

Whether treated by doctors or in the home, herbal remedies were used for all but the most severe illness with equal success or failure. Those remedies would often be applied along with a prayer for a quick recovery. However innocent the prayer may have been, the Kirk smelt the whiff of brimstone and heard diabolical spells rather than heavenly pleas for help.

Mortality rates were high and even in years of plenty food and no plague life expectancy for ordinary individuals was about 40 years. Around 25% of children died before their first birthday and 50% died before their tenth birthday. Childbirth was an especially dangerous time for women with approximately 200 out of every 1,000 births resulting in a maternal death. [1]

With older female relatives such as grandmothers helping to deliver babies and attending to sick children they were an easy target when death occurred. Of those accused of causing the death of a child by witchcraft the vast majority were relatives that had merely been helping with herbal remedies and a homely prayer in a family crisis.

---

[1] Care must be taken over these figures due to the scarcity and accuracy of records, as such they can only ever be estimates.

8. GALLOWSHIELS 1668

'her petticoats a' agape'

allowshiels in the 1600s was known as a small town north of its more important neighbour Selkirk. Created a Burgh in 1599 by the mid 17th century its population had risen to around five hundred attacted mainly by the work available in the town's three mills. The town, in common with so many in the Borders, saw several witch trials over the century. And in most of the trials the familiar pattern would be seen of the poor and the dispossessed being brought before the courts. In the case of Gallowshiels the Pringles and the Scotts predominantly sat as Commissioners. As the century wore on the sons of previous Commissioners would take the place of their fathers sitting in judgement in the witchcraft trials.

1668 was no exception. Jonet Armstrong was brought to trial with James Pringle of Buckholme, George Pringle of Torwoodlee, James Pringle of Torwoodlee, Sir James Pringle of Gallowshiels, William Scott of Gallowshiels, and Sir William Scott of Harden, acting as Commissioners. Each was either the son of a previous Commissioner or was the father of a future Commissioner.

Jonet had been known as a healer and midwife but that had been twenty years or more in the past. Now she was an old woman crippled with arthritis and going blind. Her age was not recorded for certain but she was said to be at least as old as the century itself. Always poor she was now almost destitute and eked out her life by begging for alms from neighbours and strangers alike. The giving of alms was

expected from those who could afford it and in many cases made the
difference between life and death for some. Perhaps Jonet relied on
those she had previously helped years before to remember her now
that she had fallen on hard times.

Well known round the town Jonet had lived in Gallowshiels all her
life and was described as an indweller of the town. Although an old
woman she does not appear to have had a bad reputation as there is
no note of her in previous records. She, presumably, knew who to
approach for alms and who to avoid and the townsfolk probably
looked on her, if not kindly, at least as nothing more than a nuisance.
However in the spring of 1668, for some reason that is not recorded,
that changed and Jonet suddenly became a dame of ill repute. She had
angered a neighbour in some way perhaps she had asked for some
bread and milk just one time too many, perhaps she had been refused
and had walked away muttering. Whatever the cause the neighbour
complained to the local Minister who summoned Jonet to appear
before him and the Kirk Elders.

There appears to have been some delay in Jonet appearing before the
Kirk Elders and in that time the list of offences had already started
to increase. She was not always present in the Kirk of a Sunday, she
muttered curses under her breath at her neighbours and she was
thought to have lain an illness some years previously. By the time
Jonet stood before the Kirk Elders their minds may well have been
set but unfortunately for Jonet she was to provide further proof of
her wickedness by her very appearance.

Jonet was ushered into the presence of the Minister and the Elders
dressed in the only clothes she possessed. A destitute old woman in a
dirty, tattered dress, the Minister was outraged to note that she stood
before them with '*her petticoats a' agape*'. This affront to the dignity of
the Kirk was added to the list of offences against her and armed with
the list the Minister promptly went to the local court and swore out
a plea for a trial. The inevitable train of events was set in motion and
Jonet was duly arrested and locked up in the Tolbooth.

After several days of being watched, walked and questioned Jonet could take no more and confessed her crime. Yes she was a witch, had renounced her baptism and made a pact with the Devil. The belief was that on renunciation of their Christain baptism a new witch would place one hand on her head and another onto the sole of her foot and promise the Devil everything that lay between. Jonet was noted to be so old and crippled that she could barely stand on her two legs never mind one. However this appeared to hold little sway with the Elders. Now a self confessed witch Jonet could only wait for her trial which was set for three days hence. A guilty verdict and execution was the most likely outcome however, the Devil, no doubt taking care of one of his own, had other plans and at some point over the following two days old Jonet died.

The records do not state what happened to Jonet's body but although not convicted no Kirk burial appears to have taken place. She may have received a pauper's burial but despite the lack of trial she had been labelled witch and it is more likely that her body would have been dumped. Taking her out to the hills or moorland outside the town would have involved time and effort it is more likely her body was merely cast into the Gala water.

Regardless of the fact that there had not been an actual trial, all six Commissioners claimed expenses for their time interrogating Jonet Armstrong. They each received five pounds Scots for their trouble. During the time of her imprisonment and interrogation, one shilling and sevenpence was spent on bread and ale for Jonet. Her petticoats, which had so offended the Minister, were sold for washing rags to pay the bill for her bread.

Before the Reformation the prosecution of witches along with other matters of morality was a matter for the church with the secular authorities playing a more minor role. After the Reformation however, the General Assembly of the Kirk was concerned with the entire area of social control and how this should be administered. The chaos that had reigned during the wars of the Reformation may have been, for the most part, behind them, but the Kirk was under no illusion that the Devil would attack the new faith in whatever manner he could. The morality of the common people was ripe for exploitation unless the authorities took firm control.

The Kirk wrote to the Privy Council suggesting that either the Kirk take over the jurisdiction of such matters or that the Privy Council undertake to do so. Witchcraft was not specifically outlined but either way, the Kirk wanted social control firmly embedded in the legislation of the new nation of God.

When the new criminal law was drafted in 1563 witchcraft was listed as an area for the secular authorities. However, the Kirk kept tight hold of its authority over morality. In 1567 the Parliament, heavily influenced by the Kirk debated how *'witchcraft sal be puneist and inquisition takin thereof'*. As far as the Kirk was concerned they were the lead authority in witchcraft cases with the secular courts merely the instrument by which punishment was meted out. This attitude was not challenged by the Privy Council and in 1575 the Kirk outlined its powers with regard to witchcraft *'the Kirk hath power to cognosce and decerne upon heresies, blasphemie, witchcraft and violation of the Sabbath day without prejudice always of the civill punishment'*.

During the 17th century the power and influence of the Kirk in the secular courts was further consolidated by the passing of the Act of Classes and the Test Act. In 1649 the Act of Classes was passed which gave the Kirk in Scotland a veto over those allowed to hold office, including court officials. Then in 1681 the Test Act also required any person holding office to acknowledge the supremacy of the Kirk of Scotland.

The courts that prosecuted witches might be secular but that was merely an irrelevance and it was the Kirk that would determine both guilt and punishment. The implementation of this became the established custom and practise throughout lowland Scotland. The result was that in most trials guilty verdicts and executions were the norm while in some cases, where the legal niceties has not been fully observed, the secular court authorities would ignore such technicalities and simply yield to the Kirk's rule.

To bring a suspected witch to trial involved a somewhat complicated legal process. Firstly a complaint had to be raised and the witch initially identified. Then the decision would be taken to try the suspect. The suspected witch would then be arrested and brought to trial. This process would usually start with a complaint from an individual who suspected a witch. The individual would then usually go to the Kirk Minister and complain. At this point the Minister would decide whether or not to seek a trial and would then go to the court and lodge a formal complaint. The court would then look at the evidence available, usually drawn up by the Minister, and decide whether or not to hold a trial.

The complexity of this process makes the number involved in witchcraft trials even more astonishing as, theoretically, at any point in the chain the process could be halted. There are no records showing how many initial complaints that were lodged failed to result in a full trial. However, the role of the Kirk in the process tended to ensure that once an initial complaint was laid it inevitably led to a trial. Once the Minister had been told of an offence and been given a name it was left to him to produce the evidence on which the court decided whether or not to hold a trial. The same Minister would aid in the interrogation of the suspect once they had been arrested. There was also one other crucial role early in the process which fell to the Minister. Not every individual who complained about being the victim of witchcraft named a specific witch. A general complaint of suspected witchcraft may have been made when a child was ill or food had been spoiled without the victim being absolutely sure of the perpetrator. In these cases it would be the Minister who would supply the name.

For a witchcraft case then the Minister might decide who the accused was, would list the offences against the accused, carry out an initial investigation, plead for a trial, lead the interrogation after the accused's arrest and then present the evidence against the accused witch in court. The Minister would also be called on to advise the court as to the suitability of the members of the jury.

The court system for cases of witchcraft involved several different types of courts all of which had their own specialised roles. From the lodging of the initial complaint to the passing of sentence on a convicted witch could require the involvement of more than one court at different stages of the proceedings.

The first court was that of the local Kirk sessions and Presbyteries. Although the Kirk had the authority to gather evidence and interrogate suspects they did not have any criminal jurisdiction and once a case was prepared against a suspect it would be passed onto either the Sheriff Courts, Burgh Courts, local Criminal Courts, Circuits Courts, or Court of Justiciary. The Kirk, depending on the severity of the case, would apply to the Privy Council, the Committee of Estates or the Parliament to ask for a Commission of Justiciary. This was the formal authority necessary in order for a trial to be held. Once a Commission was granted a trial could proceed.

The Sheriff Courts and Burgh Courts were the normal local courts which dealt with local crime. As witchcraft was considered a serious crime it was usually considered to be beyond their normal jurisdiction and rarely came before them. There are cases however of witch trials coming before the Sheriff courts in the Borders. It is unclear from the records exactly why this was so but it may well have been a matter of expediency as the local Sheriff courts would have dealt quickly with local cases and sent the guilty to the flames. They might also have been less scrupulous with the tedious application of legal technicalities which could, frustratingly for the local Kirk, slow proceedings down.

Local criminal courts were held under Commissions of Justiciary as issued by the Privy Council, the Committee of Estates or the Parliament. Most Scottish witchcraft trials were held in local criminal courts. These were generally convened to try one individual. These courts were most common in urban areas.

Circuit Courts held the same authority as the Court of Justiciary and travelled round the country to areas where no other suitable court existed to try witch cases. This court was most common in rural areas and carried out the greatest number of trials in the Borders. The Court of Justiciary itself was the highest criminal court in the land and was situated in Edinburgh. The Circuit Courts relied on the local nobility to act as Commissioners in witch cases.

The process between initial accusation and final sentence could be a long and arduous one.

The Kirk took its work most seriously and proceeded slowly and methodically interrogating and gathering evidence over a prolonged period of time. Once they were convinced of the guilt of the individual they had to apply for a Commission to try the witch. That in itself could take time. Not only was communication slow, especially in the winter months, but the Privy Council often took some time reading over applications for Commissions. There were also other duties to be performed by the Privy Council and despite the insistence of the Kirk a Commission to try a witch in Melrose or Coldingham may not have been a priority. The Privy Council might also ask for further evidence to be gathered which further prolonged matters. Once a Commission had been granted then further time was spent gathering the Circuit Court Commissioners.

Once a trial took place however, the proceedings could progress relatively quickly. Most witnesses that had to be called lived locally and there was rarely a defence offered. There was a problem with witnesses however. In 16th century Scotland women did not exist as far as criminal law was concerned. They were considered the equivalent of children and could not be called to give evidence in a trial. This posed a problem for the courts dealing with witchcraft cases. One of the main proofs against an individual was to be named by another witch. However, as most witches were women their evidence would be inadmissible in the courts. Other proofs and evidence were acceptable but the inability to introduce the fact that one witch had named another worried the authorities. It was well known that a witch could, on occasions, hide her Devil's Mark. What if the witch, by some trickery, tampered with the other evidence against them in a trial? Without the evidence of delation by another witch cases might fall. As the number of witchcraft trials rose so too did the concern that some witches would escape their punishment. As the 17th century beckoned, this problem was solved by the passing of a Parliamentary Act in 1591 that allowed women to give testimony in court, but only in a case involving witchcraft.

A person could be acquitted, found guilty or found not proven on some or all charges. In the case of being found guilty sentence depended on the severity of the crime but also the influence of the local Kirk. Most courts recognised that while the actions of a witch were criminal, the causes of witchcraft were spiritual and fell into the authority of the Kirk. Naturally when sentence was to be passed they turned to the Kirk for guidance. Sentence could be excommunication, banishment or exile, branding, death by burning, or death by strangulation then burning. All witches were excommunicated, although this could be for a short period of time in some instances. Some witches, mainly those with money and influential friends, managed to be exiled. Most Kirk Elders however, followed their scripture's command, 'thou shalt not suffer a witch to live'. While it was the legal responsibility of the court to pass sentence the command of the Kirk, as moral guardian, was, in almost all cases, absolute. It was rare for a court not to follow the Kirk's command and where this happened it was usually in the case of a wealthy and influential individual. Most witches were worriet then burnt.

Famine

Famine can strike for several reasons, climatic, economic, political, or a combination of factors. In the 17th century famine was to strike the Borders six times. On five of those occasions the famine would last for a single year. It would twice visit with its deadly ally plague and in 1695 it would come and stay in the Border lands for around seven years.

The 17th century was a period of cooler temperatures. This reduced the growing season across Scotland and increased pressure on existing farming areas. When a bad harvest struck and food stocks in Edinburgh ran low the city fathers would authorise the forced buying of grain from the rural hinterlands. The price offered was rarely enough for Border farmers and their own stocks were low but refusal to sell could result in grain and livestock being taken without any payment. Poverty and bad roads would also help to worsen the situation. A bad harvest in the Borders might be localised but with poor roads impassable in Autumn storms little relief could be brought in from other areas. Even when journeys could be attempted with no produce to sell the Borderers had no money to buy.

The politics of the European powers in the 17th century were frequently resolved by armies. Armies that needed fed. Official policy might have been to pay local farmers for their produce but on the ground soldiers more often than not, and frequently under orders from local commanders, just took what was necessary and who would complain? Retreating troops, of whatever side, would also use the scorched earth policy of torching fields as they went to leave no supplies for pursuing armies. Soldiers need food and they also need wages. The money to pay coming from taxes levied on all. A farmer faced with taxes would have less money to buy new stock and further compound problems.

Famine had many effects. Starvation is the most obvious and as always it was the old, the young and the sick who died first. For those who survived however a period of little food made the body susceptible to illness and disease and this could last for two or three years after the actual famine had passed. This could result in the death of stronger fitter individuals especially in prolonged periods of famine or where famine years came close together as occurred in 1644 and 1648. Famine also increased the numbers walking the roads. Unable to pay for food many would wander door to door in search of help. In some cases families would send children out in search of food possibly believing children would evoke more pity and thus be fed.

Between 1651 and 1653 the famine in Ireland was exacerbated by the presence of Cromwellian troops. Some fled to Scotland landing on the west coast and taking to the roads. Some travelled down to Dumfries and Galloway and some up to Ayrshire, Glasgow and the Clyde valley and some came across to the Borders.

Coming just a few years after the 1648 famine that had devastated the Borders they put pressure on an already fragile rural economy. Unwelcome, few were to settle long term.

Whatever the cause famine was seen as a punishment from God for sin. Where famine was localised, such as occurred in the Borders, a community could add the guilt of knowing that the famine was their own fault to the misery of starvation. Their wickedness and sinfulness causing the blight on the land.

The famine which struck the Borders in the 1690s affected the whole of Scotland and lasted for some seven years. It is estimated that as much as 15% of the population died. It has been also been estimated that around two million people died across Europe as a results of all the famines of the 17th Century.

9. JEDBURGH 1671

'ane sterving conditione'

ying just ten miles north of the Scottish Border Jedburgh had seen its fair share of destruction in the wars with the English in the 16th century as well as the cross border raids of the Rivers. It was also the site of the infamous Jethart Justice when men were hanged first and tried after. By the time the 17th century arrived it had settled down into a more peaceable town with trade starting to flourish supplied by the surrounding fertile farm land and aided by roads both north and south. But just like the other Borders towns it was not to escape the scourge of the Covenanters wars and plague and famine. Neither was it free from the witchcraft trials. Times were improving but life was still hard. By the 1670s however, the Covenanters had put away their swords and the Kirk had settled its differences with Kings and Parliaments. Famine lay over twenty years in the past and the town breathed a litle easier. A perfect time for the old enemy to strike again. This was to prove a new twist to Jethart Justice.

In the early spring of 1671 one Mary Sommerveil of Jedburgh was delated as a witch and was arrested and placed in the Tolbooth of Jedburgh. In the April she was seen at the Circuit Court who found a case against her and sent her papers up to the High Court of Justiciary in Edinburgh to be tried for the crime of witchcraft. However, in July her case was dismissed by the High Court as there was no evidence against her, no witnesses against her and she was duly released. The High Court stated 'that ther was no informatione given in aganist her nor persone com-peiring to insist aganist her ... ordaines the petitioner to be *put at libertie.'*. This triumph of justice however leaves unanswered two questions? Who named Mary and why did the Jedburgh Circuit Court find a case against her when no witnesses or evidence could be presented?

Jethart Justice – 'first hang a man syne judge him'

Justice in 17th Scotland could be and frequently was both swift and brutal. In 1603 when King James VI of Scotland succeeded to the English throne one of his first acts was to subdue the wild Border lands of the Reivers. He appointed new men to oversee Borders justice by means of a purge of the most troublesome families. Known Reivers were rounded up and hanged without trial.

It was said that in Jedburgh the authorities dealing with the Reivers 'first hang a man syne judge him', and so Jethart Justice was born. Jedburgh was to see mass hangings of many hundreds as Jethart Justice ripped the heart out of many families.

By 1610 the hangings were over as many Reiving families had either fled, been deported or died at the end of a rope. The legend of Jethart Justice would however, live on.

Mary is recorded as being delated a witch not accused. So whoever had called her witch was themselves a witch. Puzzlingly the name of the other witch is not listed. A quarrel with a spiteful neighbour could have given rise to an accusation of witchcraft sufficient to cause the initial arrest but that was a very different thing from being delated by another witch. Have the records been lost? However, when no witnesses or evidence were produced to corroborate the accusation against Mary, why was she not released? Why did the local court send her case up to Edinburgh? Most Borders towns preferred to have as little to do with Edinburgh as possible but as the century moved on and concerns over legal procedure became more prevalent some cases were sent up to the higher courts. But with no evidence against her the local authorities must have known that Edinburgh would order Mary's release. Delated as a witch used to be proof positive but with no supporting evidence did Jedburgh hesitate and pass the buck to Edinburgh or was something more sinister going on?

The situation becomes even more strange with another case of Jedburgh being ordered to release a suspected warlock, George Guislet. Yet again George had been arrested and yet again there were no witnesses against him. George was released in July 1671 just one week after Mary under the orders of the Justiciary Court of Edinburgh. The court records, *'George Guislet imprisoned for witchcraft at the last circuit at Jedburgh is sett at liberty because none compears to insist'*. And again the questions arise, why was a case found against George when no witnesses existed? And had George been the one to delate Mary, frustratingly the records do not say. But with two arrests in Jedburgh with no witnesses or evidence the questions simply multiply. What was going on in Jedburgh? With no witnesses or evidence against Mary and George there was only one authority that had the power to order an arrest in such a case; the Kirk.

An unsupported accusation from a neighbour might have sparked an investigation but with no evidence or witnesses would have quickly been dismissed. Most records of petty squabbles between neighbours show just that outcome with the accuser often chided for their ill temper and in some instances cases were brought against accusers for slander where the word witch had been uttered. For Mary, and later George, to land in the Tolbooth when the original witch that had delated them was not only not in custody but unnamed was suspect. Admittedly the original witch could have died by why was their name not recorded? Arrested on the word of the Minister Mary sat out four months in gaol while the local authorities tried to find evidence against her. Interestingly no witch pricker was brought to brod her for the Devil's Mark, perhaps that was a step too far even for the local Sheriff. The records do not state what crimes Mary was alleged to have committed it only states she was *'accused of witchcraft'*. No mention of laying of sickness or any of the other usual accusations are recorded and Mary, it seems, had no trouble in finding an advocate to draw up a petition for her.

The papers for Mary's release signed in July, state that she was in *'ane sterving conditione'* and this gives a further detail to her case.

When arrested individuals, or their relatives and friends, would have to pay for the accused's upkeep in the gaol. If Mary was, after four months in the Tolbooth, starving, either her friends and family had abandoned her, or were no longer able to support her. She may also have had no means of support but herself and it was not uncommon for unsupported women to sell everything they had, including occasionally their bodies, to buy food while awaiting trial. Several of the justices complained that women sent for trial often appeared before them in little more than rags having had to literally sell the clothes off their backs in order not to starve to death.

In George's case no mention is made of starvation so it may be that George had the help that Mary did not or that he was not held as long in gaol. Whatever means Mary had at her disposal she also had an advocate to pay. Had the cost of a lawyer reduced her to starvation? Possibly but Mary obviously thought it well worth the price.

Whatever the reasons for Mary's starvation when Jedburgh had sent her papers to Edinburgh they had not done so willingly. Mary's petition clearly stated the lack of evidence against her and her willingness to appear before any court to answer for the charges against her. Her appeal had reached the Privy Council in Edinburgh. Jedburgh had not merely sent Mary's papers to Edinburgh, the papers had been demanded. Ordering her release and that of George Guislet, Edinburgh was in no doubt there was no evidence against either of them and Jedburgh was ordered to release them immediately. There is no record that George petitioned against his own imprisonment so it may be he owed his release to Mary's determination to clear her own name. Had Mary been less determined both she and George might have fallen victims to Jethart Justice.

The records do not show any investigation into the Jedburgh authorities illegal imprisonment of Mary and George. Perhaps they have been lost, or perhaps the Edinburgh authorities, while willing to act when compelled by an advocate, left well alone where Jethart Justice was concerned.

A strong personality can be a double edged sword and it may well have been Mary's strong nature that had riled the local Minister against her in the first place. Be that as it may, she was released and disappeared from the official records.

So what awaited an acquitted witch on their return to the community? Many were not unknown to the Kirk having been in trouble on more than one occasion before their arrest. Already outcast possibly due to a sharp tongue and definitely after an accusation of witchcraft and a spell in the Tolbooth, most would find themselves free but destitute. Several parish records tell of the fate of those witches released after paying fines or even those acquitted but still suspected in their communities. Homes left weeks previously in exchange for gaol were no longer welcoming and those without family to support them, or in some cases without a family willing to support them, often found themselves homeless. Unable to get work they would soon turn to begging and while fear of retribution would earn them a crust from most as summer turned to autumn and autumn to winter food and shelter would become more and more scarce. A Borders winter spent out of doors with little or no food and shelter would test the strongest of constitutions let alone someone who had spent time in gaol having undergone torture and ill treatment.

Even for those able to stay in their communities the welcome was far from warm. Acquitted by the courts was one thing but suspected by your neighbours of having got off by some diabolical means was quite another. Fear would keep most away but muttered suspicion would feed distrust on one side and resentment on another and when any disaster struck again a further round of accusations and arrests could be expected. Many records show the same names recurring time and again with the same individuals having records that stretch over twenty years.

Flitting to another village or town was rarely an option but even when it was tried the results were seldom much better. Having moved from a known, even if hostile, environment to an unknown one was a daunting task. Ordinary people rarely moved from their home town or village in 17th century Borders and those that did, merely moved to the next town. Movement of farm goods to markets ensured that anyone attempting to escape a bad reputation would most likely be seen by someone from their home town or village. Once named as a witch the new town would view an incomer with double suspicion, now known as a witch they could only have moved for one reason to practice witchcraft. Any out of the ordinary occurrence, any illness and the incomer was the first name on everyone's lips.

Life for the community after a trial could also be a testing time. Now that the excitement of the trial was over and the guilty had been duly disposed of life in the community returned back to normal. The court had left, or been dissolved. The witch was dead but did more lurk in unsuspecting corners?

Had those that had died really been guilty? No-one could voice any doubts: what doubt the Minister? No one dared whisper, for what part had they played? But no they had been guilty, after all they had confessed and been executed. But then again hadn't they recanted their confession?...

And what of the accusers? For those few brief weeks they had tasted power as never before, would they be content to slide back into obscurity? For a brief moment they had held the town enthralled to their tales. The Minister, the Magistrate, the Sheriff, all had sat entranced hanging on their every word. They had been the powerful ones and what a power of life and death even. Could they go back to being ordinary, could they return from a position of power to the day to day drudgery of their everyday lives?

Had their stories been true? If true then there was the belief that they had done their duty: they had consigned a witch to eternal damnation but that too could prove a burden. For ordinary people hell was not a great theological concept but a real place. A place that you might well go to when you died. For those who attended the Kirk they were reminded of this fact in almost every weekly sermon. Didn't the Minister explain in detail the torments awaiting those who denied God? Belief in hell was universal. Hell was a place of ever lasting torment: a place of pain and unimaginable suffering that went on for all eternity. And this was the place to which they had consigned the witches. Even those of the strongest constitution might have cause for some reservations at their actions.

And what of those who had embellished their stories? What did their conscience say to them in the wee small hours? Did they lie awake at night contemplating the horror of their actions? After the trial of a witch many were seen to attend the Kirk most assiduously for several weeks but soon that too would slip and lives would fade back into normality. Some who had given evidence had profited: a piece of land had come their way, or compensation for a dead pig was awarded by the courts, but that too could have its downside. Resentment came from those who had been equally affected by the witch but had not gained, as well as from the plain jealous. There were also those who had not been witnesses but had still been seen to profit. The usual ones had had their snouts in the trough selling coal and tar to burn the witch and providing food and lodgings to the courts and their officials. They walked about with fat purses while others scratched their heads and wondered who would pay the bill for the gaolers wages. Resentments simmered under the surface and not just in those feeling hard done by.

What of those families who had lost a mother, a wife, a sister? They had to rebuild their lives. For those that had abandoned the witch to her fate was left the guilt of having failed in their duty to a loved one. Those who had managed to stand by their relative faced disapproval and condemnation from Kirk and community alike. Tainted by association, suspicion could become lodged in a neighbour's mind. Even for those whose relation had died due to torture or ill treatment in gaol, or who had simply been unable to withstand their treatment and had committed suicide, the name witch stuck. When ill fortune struck the community again voices muttered and old tales were revived. Was this an attack from new witches or was it the revenge of the family of the old witch that had been put to death? A witch's child might easily grew up to be a witch themselves or might already be one. What powers might they have, what revenge might they wreck and on whom?

A witchcraft trial had one last gift to bestow on the community, fear. And that fear could have two heads. The Devil had attacked them before, he could attack them again at any minute. No longer could illness be viewed as natural it was forever more to be seen as the work of diabolical witches. The world was a frightening place where witches attacked the Godly and threatened their children. The Minister in his pulpit had become a more terrifying figure, ever warning of the attacks of witches and ever accusing.

Not all witch executions sat well with communities and after the dust had settled more sober heads prevailed. How could an argument over bread have led to a burning? Those executed had been known, had been ordinary. If they could be accused, so could anyone.

Communities that had seen a trial were uneasy places in the immediate aftermath. Free from witches they might have been but suspicion, resentment and fear had been left in their place.

The frozen body of an emaciated woman, reputed to be that of Mary Sommerveil, was found on the 23 December 1671 on the road south out of Jedburgh. As a witch, even one only suspected of witchcraft, she would not be given Christian buried in the Kirkyard. Burial by the road was thought to bring ill luck to travellers and no-one was found willing to do the task. The body was stripped and dumped in the Jed Water.

10. STOBO 1679

'the dumb man in the correction house'

The lands of Stobo changed hands between the Kirk and the nobility many times from the Reformation until the 17th century. The start of the 17th century saw the lands given by James VI first to Sir John Maitland of Thirlestane, then the Duke of Lennox and then in 1608 to the Archbishop of Glasgow. In 1613 the Archbishop granted the lands in a charter to James Tweedie. The lands then passed into the ownership of John Murray of Halmyre in 1619 and Stobo was to remain Murray land for the next 72 years.

Lying just five miles from Peebles, Stobo benefited from the good pasture, clean water and fair roads to Edinburgh and the west. Stobo, unlike it larger neighbour Peebles, had only experienced one witchcraft trial in the previous fifty years when, in the autumn of 1679, two men from Stobo would be brought to trial not for being warlocks but for the equally heinous crime of having consulted with one.

The Witchcraft Act of 1563 was quite specific it outlawed both witches and those who consulted with witches. The central belief of the Kirk was that a witch had renounced her baptism and made a covenant with the Devil. By consulting with a known witch an individual was therefore condoning that act and by seeking help from a servant of the Devil, rather than from a servant of God, was challenging God's authority. In the eyes of the law and the Kirk any such individual was equally as guilty as any witch.

William and James Stewart, who were brothers, were merchants in Stobo. Some time in October 1678 they decided to visit a warlock, the dumb man in Edinburgh. This was no drunken spree or spur of the moment decision to visit a local witch but was a rational and planned act. The brothers had to leave their business, travel to Edinburgh, pay for food and overnight lodgings, pay for stabling for their horses and pay to see the dumb man. No small undertaking and certainly outwith the pocket of most people at that time.

This visit to Edinburgh was merely the latest consultation the brothers had undertaken over a period of several months. Whatever the brothers were seeking the local witches had been unable to deliver and they sought help from the notorious dumb warlock.

The dumb man is not named in the records but is listed as a known warlock. The question must be asked, if he was a known warlock, why had he not been executed? Why was he being held in a house of correction? Warlock he may have been but as a dumb man he may have been classed as a lunatic. He would therefore probably have escaped the ropes and flames but been imprisoned for life in the lunatic asylum, the correction house, rather than the gaol. He may possibly have been allowed some visitors from time to time such as family members, if he had any, but for William and James, two strangers, to visit was extremely risky. They would have had to have paid the wardens for access to the man and this could have set tongues wagging. If doubts had already been raised when they had left Stobo this visit would have increased misgivings as the nature of their trip.

However the suspicion arose, on their return to Stobo they were reported to the Minister and called before the Elders to account for themselves. The Minister and Elders noted that they had visited and consulted with several witches and charmers and convinced that there was a case to answer called for a Commission. What the Minister thought about his two parishioner's belief in witches is not recorded. The Privy Council was busy over the winter and the

Commission was not received until the spring. William and James were arrested and interrogated over the summer as to their conduct and a trial was finally set for September.

The indictment dittay lists several offences against each brother *'consulting with witches, charmers and such as have familiar spirites particularly the dumb man in the correction house of Edinburgh'*. It was further noted however that neither brother had their own familiar spirites and so were not thought of as witches themselves.

On the 26 September the trial began and was deserted that very day. William and James were set free. This was not the same as an acquittal but meant that the trial had been abandoned as there was no case to answer. If the evidence collected by the Minister was enough to convince the Privy Council of the need for a Commission and a trial why then suddenly were the local Commissioners of the opposite opinion that there was no case to answer? The clue may lie in the difference between the Privy Council in Edinburgh and the local Commissioners.

While the records that list the date of the trial remain intact and the records that state that the diet had been deserted remain intact, the record of the names of the local Commissioners, that decided there was no case to answer, have been lost. Neither William nor James denied their actions. The evidence against them was overwhelming: they had consulted a warlock. There was no legal reason to stop the trial. The only people who had the authority to stop the trial were the unnamed Commissioners. But why? What could William and James have said in open court that the local Commissioners wanted left unsaid?

The usual sentence for an individual found guilty of consulting with a known witch was to be worriet and then burnt. William and James left court completely exonerated. Both continued to successfully trade within the town for several years before eventually moving to Edinburgh as wealthy merchants.

The execution of witches was more or less a foregone conclusion. The scriptures admonished *'thou shalt not suffer a witch to live'* (Exodus 22:18) and God's elect followed scripture to the letter. In Scotland the main method of execution for witches was to be 'worriet' or throttled and then burnt. For those who did not meet this gruesome fate they could be excommunicated, flogged, branded, exiled, hanged and, for some poor unfortunates, they could be burnt alive without the mercy of having been strangled first. The latter fate tended to be reserved for those intransigent individuals who, as well as their acts of witchcraft, refused to ask for forgiveness and revelled in their wickedness.

After sentence was passed the witch would be admonished by the local Minister and her soul prayed over. A pyre would be built in a public place such as the local market square and everyone would be told to attend the execution. The pyre usually consisted mainly of wood with some coal and tar used to help the burning. The wood used was always freshly cut as superstition dictated that one who had given up or sold wood for a burning would be haunted by the witch thereafter and have nothing but bad luck. In wet weather wood would be cut and stored usually where the witch was being held as again no-one wanted even to store the wood. Rope and any other materials used would often be brought in from outwith the town.

In some cases the witch would be burnt in a tar barrel instead of being tied to a stake. This usually involved tying the dead body of the worriet witch into a barrel half filled with tar which was then set alight. Local superstition often preferred this method as it was felt that the barrel was a better container and there was less possibility of an escape at the last moment. Most Kirk Ministers vehemently opposed this reasoning explaining to the ignorant mob that the Devil could not defeat God and rescue 'his' witch. Depending on the mood of the mob, and the amount of ale consumed, the theological argument was not always completely believed. The low number of barrel burnings was most likely down to the cost of burning a good barrel.

On the morning of the execution the witch would be roused at dawn. Long hair would be hacked off with a razor for ease of strangulation. The witch would then be put in a hair shift. If the witch had been brodded this could open up old wounds. The shift was then painted with tar to help with the burning. The witch then had their shoes removed to appear penitent and barefoot before God. Their hands would be bound behind their back and they would then be marched through the town by two of the Baillie's men.

Once they had reached the place of execution sentence would then be repeated and the local Minister would usually preach a sermon reminding the townsfolk of the wickedness of witches and of the damnation and hellfire that awaited them. The executioner then stepped forward. This may have been a local man but in some of the smaller villages would have had to have been fetched in from one of the larger towns.

After a final exhortation from the Minister the executioner went to work. Two Baillie's men held onto the witch's arms and would force her into a kneeling position. With the witch in the kneeling position and held fast the executioner would approach. He would then slip a knotted rope over the witch's head and twist it round the neck until it was tight. He might then put one of his knees in the small of the witch's back to get a good purchase and use the witch's bound hands as a resting place for his foot. They often rested their body weight on the witch's bound hands but as she was held fast by the Baillie's man this would pull down on the arms and could break both shoulders. Once in a comfortable position he would start to twist the rope. Occasionally a small piece of wood would be inserted between the victim's neck and the rope and the wood was then twisted to increase pressure. It could take a few minutes to die depending on the strength of the executioner, his experience and the amount of 'give' in the rope.

Most were unconscious within ten to fifteen seconds and inexperienced executioners or, in the case of multiple executions, those who were tired, might then suppose the witch to be dead and deliver them onto the pyre or into the tar barrel.

All this time the witch was facing the assembled throng of people who watched as she was throttled. Those who looked away were noted and duly admonished by the Minister. The spectacle was a truly gruesome one. The face would start to swell up and the lips, tips of the ears and nose would take on a blueish tinge as the blood supply was cut off. The eyes would bulge in their sockets and the tongue would protrude from the mouth. There was usually a frothy mucous streaming from both mouth and nostrils and the on lookers would hear the victim choking. Unable to move to aid themselves the victims fingers and hands would twist and turn in the ropes cutting themselves in the process.

After the victim was dead, or appeared dead, the body was tied onto the pyre, or into the barrel, and burnt. If the victim was not dead and came to on the fire, this was seen not as evidence that they had not been worriet properly but as a last feeble attempt by the witch to escape justice. The fact that they did not escape was evidence of the Devil's abandonment of the witch in her last agonies.

The execution of a witch served a two fold purpose: it consigned an evil doer to the flames but just as importantly it served to illustrate to the local populace the power of the true faith and the trickery of the Devil. This was a creature who had promised his followers everything their hearts had desired and he had abandoned them like the liar he was. He had been proved false and wicked and had abandoned them to their fate. It was for this reason that Kirk Elders required everyone's presence at an execution. This was also pertinent where several witches were executed together. After the death of the first of their colleagues, they were confronted by the falsity of the Devil and called on to witness his treachery. For those who had not confessed, a final demand that they admit their guilt was demanded.

Execution could be a costly business and after the witch was disposed of the costs of the trial and execution had to be paid. Typical costs covered everything from messengers and coals, to ale and rope.

Coal	5 merks
Tar barrels	12 shillings
Ropes	7 shillings
Messengers	45 shillings
Executioner	£7 15 shillings
Baillie's men ale	10 shillings
Pricker	£5
Commission	£ 8 12 shillings
Candles for watching witch	15 shillings
Food and bedding for witch	5 shillings

However, not everyone sentenced to death went immediately to the flames. A common delaying tactic was for a woman to 'plead her belly', claiming to be pregnant. The hope was that after several months the locals might, after having had to pay for the witch's keep for so long, once what money the witch had was gone, be disposed to merely send her on her way rather than face the expense of an execution.

There was also the idea that a few extra months might give time for an appeal for, at least, a lesser sentence if not the overturning of the original verdict. However this was a scheme that was fraught with danger. For those who were pregnant, there was no guarantee of release and indeed some towns after having had to pay for the maintenance of a witch for a further six months or so often vented their anger the only way they could. They dispensed with the 'mercy' of having the witch worriet and she might find herself facing the flames alive and fully conscious.

For those who were not expecting the problem was how to get pregnant before the nine months were up. While there were those who took advantage, sexually, of those accused of witchcraft they were in fact fewer that might be imagined. Most men were too sacred of witches and their evil magic to go anywhere near them. Those who were God fearing were repulsed by them and their wickedness.

Those of a less holy nature were still superstitious and subsequently genuinely afraid. Witches, after all, could make you impotent or shrivel your manhood. So finding a guard who would oblige was not easy. Those male friends and family members who had not fled in fear or disgust might help but had to get past the guards first and then not get caught. Some, no doubt, would have tried but the risk of capture and subsequent punishment as a witch themselves would have made them few and far between.

For those who were pregnant the fate of their baby was not a happy one. The child was removed moments after birth and given into the care of the parish. But what parish wanted the child of a convicted witch in their midst? Indeed many babies removed by a midwife were found to have no where to go. Few female friends or relatives were willing to face being ostracised by their communities for having taken the child in and yet an unclaimed child would die if not cared for. For those children who were taken in they would grow up a figure of fear and condemnation. Treatment would have been harsh and basic care minimal such that many would not see their fifth year. For those that survived into adulthood life was hard. They were, in many cases, excluded from all apects of normal community life and if the cry of witch was raised again in their town or village theirs was the first name on everyone's lips.

The Kirk, so eager to condemn the mother, was less enthusiatis in the care of the child. No records exist detailing any instances of the Kirk caring for these children. Parish care in practical terms was meaningless. Children orphaned by the death of an ordinary mother and with no family would be placed in the care of a local family and their basic upkeep paid by the Kirk until they were old enought to earn a living at around seven or eight. No such luxury was afforded the child of an executed witch. No Kirk funds were made available. Despite the estate of a witch being forfeit to the Crown, even where monies were left over, after the payment of expenses, nothing was set aside for the care of any children. Rumours abound of babes left out on the hills to perish in the cold Borders winter. Even those dying of natural causes were frequently denied Christian burial by the Kirk.

While care must always be taken when making comparisons, especially with incomplete records, it is illuminating to note that per head of population Scotland executed around ten times as many witches as England.

Edinburgh and the Lothians had the highest number of witch cases in Scotland. This was due partly as East Lothian contained the main shipping ports for Scotland and as such, saw many ships lost, these disasters often being blamed on witches. Edinburgh as the capital had the highest courts so many of the trials in Edinbugh were actually of witches from other areas of Scotland. Edinburgh and the Lothians therefore were not typical of the rest of Scotland.

Apart from Edinburgh and the Lothians, the Kirk in the Borders presided over the trial and execution of more witches than in any other area of Scotland.

11. SELKIRK 1700

'the drier ye are, the better ye'll burn'

As the century started to draw to a close so the number of witch trials and execution started to reduce. Magistrates and lawyers became aware of the number of confessions that were being retracted and gradually became less than convinced of the rigour of some of the proofs being offered in many trials. Possible miscarriages of justice which had increased as the number of trials had increased worried some as they feared they could undermine the legal system as a whole. This was compounded by several witch prickers who were found to be frauds. Pricking for the Devil's mark was no longer used as evidence of witchcraft and confession under torture also fell from favour due to the large number of retractions that had occurred. Procedures in the interrogation and investigation of suspected witches had been tightened over the century but abuses still occurred and innocents were still burnt in market places and town squares.

What was not in doubt however was a belief in witchcraft: that it did indeed exist. This view, being held more steadily in Scotland than most other European countries, remained steadfast. The problem was not whether or not witches existed or that they committed the crime of witchcraft, everyone knew and believed both to be true. Rather the problem was how to prove it. The world was changing and the debates and disputes on witchcraft continued. Most arguments revolved round how to prove witchcraft within an increasingly sophisticated legal system. Some individuals questioned whether this was a matter for the courts at all but was better left to church authorities.

A few lone voices were starting however, to question the existence of witches at all. Alarmed by this apparent lapse of faith most churches throughout Europe recognised that to counter such blasphemous ideas witchcraft trials needed to be beyond reproach. The rigour of the case brought against a witch could not be in doubt. Reform was needed. The Scottish Kirk combined therefore with the legal establishment to tighten the trial procedures to ensure competent verdicts for both spiritual and temporal reasons.

This process started in 1661-2 after the great witch hunt of that period which involved over six hundred and sixty individuals over four Scottish counties. The trials were so numerous and the death toll was so large that abuses came readily to light. These abuses included the unauthorised arrest of suspects, the use of torture without a warrant to carry out the same, pricking suspects without a warrant and the use of walking and watching suspects who were illegally held. Guilty verdicts had been reached and executions had been rapidly carried out but not without disquiet being voiced by many. Kirk zeal to secure convictions was seen, by some, as an opportunity for the local Kirk to get rid of some trouble makers while terrorising others.

After these abuses, and the public criticisms they raised, there was a gradual change in how cases were conducted. The authorities started to take more control over cases, the use of torture and pricking reduced and a more stringent use of evidence as proof was initiated.

As in all matters that emanate from the centre it often takes time to percolate to rural areas and the conduct of witchcraft trials in the Borders was no exception. The local clergy were well aware of the continuing and steadfast belief in witchcraft prevalent in Scottish society. While the judiciary might trouble themselves over legal niceties the Borders clergy continued as before encouraging a robust level of investigation and interrogation. While the argument over proving the gainsayers wrong, in the matter of the existence of witches, occupied the higher echelons of the Kirk, on the ground local Presbyteries stubbornly retained their own methods of interrogation often with the tacit approval of the Kirk hierarchy. On this occasion however, they were on the losing side and the judiciary, with their insistence on rigorous evidential based trials, won out and in 1736 had the law changed.

The courts conscious of what they could and could not prove opted for a new Act that repealed the 1563 Act but outlawed any person who '*pretend to exercise or use any kind of Witchcraft, Sorcery, Inchantment, or Conjuration, or undertake to tell Fortunes, or pretend, from his or her Skill or Knowledge in any occult or crafty Science, foretune telling,'*. By repealing the 1563 Act, in theory witchcraft was no longer illegal. In practise however, witches and witchcraft, their detection and punishment were now solely under the jurisdiction of the Kirk.

During the 17th century, most witchcraft trials in the Borders were local trials. The local clergy rarely sent their witches to Edinburgh for trial and only ever bothered with the authorities in Edinburgh to get the most basic necessary legal permissions. This however proved to be their very undoing. Obtaining a Commission to try witches, locals then went ahead to arrest, investigate, interrogate and try witches. In their enthusiasm to bring the guilty to trial, warrants were not always obtained for those other than the main suspect. Torture was often used without permission and in some cases those found not guilty or not proven would often simply not be released. In some cases the trial was simply held again with the same evidence presented to the same jury. If one witch had been found guilty this could then be brought as new evidence against the accused. There are no cases noted where a second not guilty or not proven verdict was returned. As the central authorities started to take a greater interest in the trials however, there irregularities came to light. As the laxity of the Borders trials became known the authorities insisted on a greater degree of compliance with the correct procedures.

The issue of torture was a thorny one for the courts. Torture was a perfectly acceptable method by which to obtain confessions in many cases of witchcraft. The problem was the use of torture without permission. In 1662 the Privy Council noted that many innocent persons had been executed as a result of confessions obtained under torture. These persons having retracted their confessions just before being executed. To the courts this was, at the very least, proof of possible innocence and an embarrassment to the legal system. The Kirk however, took a different view. Retraction was further proof of the wickedness of the Devil and the perfidiousness of witches. It inflamed the crowds with false notions and was the reason why accused witches should not be allowed to speak before being executed.

As a result of these dubious executions, after 1662, torture was illegal unless permission was granted by the Privy Council and was to be used with the utmost care. While there is abundant evidence of its continuing illegal use in the Borders as late as 1698, its overall use did decrease. Permissions for the use of torture became harder to obtain, just cause had to be shown, and as a result confessions became more difficult to obtain leading to higher rates of acquittal.

As the century wound on there was also an increased desire to test the evidence brought before the courts. Scottish courts allowed witches a defence, although few could afford the fees of an advocate. Nevertheless advocates ,when present, started to question the proofs brought against suspected witches. Had a bewitched child not been sick from natural causes? Was a witness truthful in their testimony of a quarrel? This was a turning point for many. However, in many local trials in the Borders the problem was not who could afford to pay for an advocate but where could an advocate be found who was willing to take on their case. The local advocate might well be the brother or son of the local Kirk Minister who was in charge of the investigation. And while rigour of evidence might hold sway in Edinburgh, the Kirk was master in the Borders. Faced with the choice of challenging the local Kirk establishment or taking on a suspected witch as a client, and with the still prevalent view that witches existed, few advocates stepped forward. Again the Borders held out longer than most regions but eventually advocates from Edinburgh and the Lothians came down to local trials and the central authorities moved greater numbers of trials to Edinburgh. Defence advocates challenging evidence became more routine and acquittal rates again rose.

It must be remembered however, that it was not the central authorities or advocates that decided the guilt or innocence of a witch. That remained with the jury of local individuals. Jury selection was on the grounds of good character. Good character was decided by the local Kirk session. The prosecuting Minister then had an inbuilt bias in the jury. All the legal procedures in the land, and all the fancy advocates from Edinburgh could not, in many cases, influence a jury to find a suspect innocent. A jury's logic, if cruel in its consequences, was as least consistent. Everyone knew witchcraft existed. The Minister suspected witch craft. The Minister had a suspect arrested. The Minister interrogated the suspect. The Minister produced evidence that showed the suspect's guilt, including a confession. Therefore, the suspect was guilty. If the defence advocates were to be believed, then the witch was innocent, and the Minister must have been wrong. For a long time that was a step too far for many juries in rural Borders. However, as more and more trials were carried out with more and more evidence being challenged, the weight of opinion from advocates and judges tipped the balance in favour of the law and the Kirk lost out.

With a refusal to allow torture, a reduction in confessions and an increase in advocates questioning evidence the witchcraft trials was becoming meaningless. The belief in witchcraft remained as strong as ever, especially amongst the Kirk, but the courts were no longer the place in which to punish the guilty.

The end of witchcraft trials did not however mean an end to witchcraft accusations. Abandoned by the judiciary, local communities were left to find their own solutions to the problems of witches in their midst. In the Borders, as in some other areas of Scotland, the local solution was simple. Lynch the witches. Accusations were made, Kirk Ministers investigated, torture was applied and then witches were worriet, burnt, hanged, drowned and stoned to death. No records exist of any arrests made in the Borders for these murders. Kirk involvement varied from parish to parish. At its most benign would be an investigation into any accusation levelled against a suspect, whilst at its most malign would come the exhortation from the pulpit, '*thou shalt not suffer a witch to live*'.

In 1700, the last recorded witch execution took place in the Borders in Selkirk. Meg Lawson, a local woman, had been tried and found guilty of '*foul wytchraft*'. The tide had been turning against the trials for some time but came too late for Meg. She was executed before a large and noisy crowd who were, as one visiting Minister remarked, '*showing great drunkenness and were much given to abusing all around including the clergy*'. Meg was to prove a great afternoons entertainment for them.

Selkirk in 1700 was becoming a thriving merchant town. The century past had seen turbulent times with the battle of Philiphaugh still a raw memory to many. However, there had also been the incorporation of many of the town's craft guilds and it seemed that the violent old days were behind Selkirk. The new century loomed promising trade and wealth as Selkirk looked to markets both north and south. But for every new merchants house there were equally back wynds with low mean cottages. And below the confident air of the new times, old superstitions still ran deep.

Selkirk had seen its fair share of witchcraft trials throughour the century with as many as twenty having faced the rope and the flame. Determined as any Border town to drive out the Devil changes in procedure handed down from Edinburgh were viewed with a mixture of suspicion and disrespect. Selkirk felt itself quite capable of dealing with its own without interference from the central authorities.

Meg Lawson was a familiar figure round the town. A healer, she was frequently consulted over child birth and in cases of sickness in children. As ever this could prove to be a dangerous profession and for Meg more so than most as she had a certain reputation. Meg, was a convicted witch.

First tried in 1662, she had confessed to being a witch. For some reason she had escaped the flames that time. Had she shown remorse, had she promised to return to the Kirk? Whatever had happened, she had served her punishment and then returned to her life in the town. In 1700 however, she was rearrested. The charges were familiar, illness of a child, but then a startling accusation of metamorphosis was laid. Meg, it seemed, had the power to turn herself into a mouse. And was it as that mouse that she had crept into homes to lay sickness on children? This seems far fetched. Invited into homes to help with child birth or to heal a sick bairn she had ample opportunity to cast her spells. What need had she to change into a mouse? And yet the story of the mouse remained. Was the Kirk worried that she might not be found guilty? Meg was tried alone not as part of a larger scare in the community. So was this a genuine case of witchcraft or was the Kirk tidying up from a previous error? Was the mouse story added to ensure a guilty verdict? Metamorphosis accusations were not unknown in Scotland but were certainly very rare and almost always resulted in a guilty verdict. Whatever the truth of the matter, mouse or no mouse Meg was found guilty again and this time would face the flames.

The great time of burnings was drawing to a close and Meg's guilt appeared no more solid that the last time, so what had changed? True this was a second offence. The Kirk, no doubt embarassed that it had not secured an execution in the previous trial, had not changed its attitude. But one thing had changed and that was Meg herself. No longer remorseful, possibly, but no longer young, definitely. An old woman, on her own, accused of laying sickness on a child Meg was unfortunate in that she fitted the Kirk's stereotype of the old witch perfectly. The old ways were indeed drawing to a close and the Kirk knew it but they would go out with a flourish supplied by Meg.

The cell was, no doubt, cold that morning despite the summer sun when Meg rose for the last time. In a thin hair shift, bare foot and bare headed and with her hands bound behind her Meg had the noose placed around her neck. The crowd outside had waited all morning for Meg. Passing the time in the town's various ale shops, they were getting restless when she finally appeared. Accompanied by the Baillie's men, she was led up the Kirk Wynd accompanied by the prayers of the Minister that were almost drowned out by the shouts and comments of the crowd.

At the foot of the Foul Brig Port Meg stumbled and begged for a drink from the fetid pool that gave the brig its name. 'Na, na, na' said the hangman, 'The drier ye are, the better ye'll burn'. At this piece of wit a great cheer went up from the crowd. Pulled to her feet Meg was dragged up to Gallows Knowe and forced to her knees. The Minister, puffing slightly, arrived and exhorted her to, at last, accept her fate and consign her soul to God. The crowd leaned forward silent eager for some more spectacle and Meg did not disappoint. She raised her head and with her hair wild about her muttered something under her breath. Too soft for the crowd to hear yet loud enough and wicked enough for the Minister to blanch and take a step back. An excited thrill went through the crowd. The Minister recovered himself and nodded to the Baillie. Two men stepped forward and held Meg's arms as the hangman slipped a small piece of wood into the noose and tightened it quickly around Meg's neck. A quiet gurgling could be heard but didn't last long. Meg had been in prison a long time and there wasn't much fight left in her old body. She quickly slipped away. Her lifeless body was dragged to the pyre and a couple of strokes of the tar brush applied before the fire was solemnly lit. The Minister started his sermon. A sudden breeze caught the flames and the fire roared to life echoed by a great roar from the crowd. The Minister started again to be met by more abuse and a flying neep that just missed his ear. Glaring at his disreputable flock, he gave up on the soul of Meg Lawson and turned tail.

De lanijs et phitonicis mu-
lieribus ad illustrissimum principem dominū Sigismūdum
archiducem austrie tractatus pulcherrimus

12. CONCLUSION

'a lingering memory'

So what happened in the Borders between 1600 and 1700? Why were witches seen in every town and village? What drove Kirk Ministers and Elders to preside over and participate in the interrogation and torture of local women and men?

The pattern of witch allegations in Scotland was not consistent. East Lothian has the dubious record of having the highest numbers of accusations, trials and executions. With its proximity to the capital, its coast line and the shipping intercourse between Scotland and the continent, this is not too surprising. However, the high numbers in the Borders area are more difficult to understand.

Between 1600 and 1700 some three hundred and fifty two known trials of witches were officially recorded in the Borders area. It has been estimated that the true figure may be even higher. As these are only the figures for official trials many more accusations must have been made that did not make it to the courts for one reason or another. With a population of only around seventy thousand this denotes a higher than average number of accusations. During this hundred year period almost every area in Scotland was awash with witch trials, although this was predominantly a lowland phenomenon.

The accusations and trials tended to occur in distinct periods e.g. 1629, 1649, 1661. While this pattern is seen in the Borders there is also a consistent number of cases being brought forward throughout the centrury. Between the main periods of high activity, the Borders could always be relied on to be bringing one or two cases when the rest of the country was relatively quite. Why should the Borders have such a high rate of cases within a relatively low population? And why, when the apparent threat of witchcraft was dormant in the rest of the country, did the Borders continue to produce and send victims to the flames?

The Borders was, like many parts of Scotland at the time, an intensely rural area where life was lived on the edge and so one poor harvest, or a cow going sick could result in death. The line for many rural poor between life and death was a thin one especially for the young, the old and the already sick. Women caring for the ill, or helping as midwives were open to accusation. As women were, predominantly, in control of the households food supply they were also those best placed to curdle a neighbour's milk or spoil a friend's ale. However, rural life was equally harsh across Scotland and risks of illness and spoilt foods were not particular to the Borders. So while doubtless a contributory factor to the accusations of witch this does not explain the higher than average rates of accusation, trials and executions.

Difficult as life was in many Borders towns and villages this was stretched to the limit by five outbreaks of plague and six instances where the harvest failed causing widespread famine in the one hundred years between 1600 and 1700. If crops had failed again and plague had returned someone must be to blame. The new century might bring the Enlightenment to Edinburgh but before that could be reached the Borders struggled to comprehend their lives in face of mounting disasters.

There was also the geography of the land. By its very nature the Borders had borne the brunt of the frequent wars between Scotland and England. The constant and continual uncertainty and proximity of death and destruction would have played their part in the local psyche. The dark and seemingly uncontrollable forces of war might have become mirrored in many communities by the apparent existence of the equally dark and uncontrollable forces of witchcraft. Here again a comparison is useful. Witchcraft accusations and trials in Galloway, another area no stranger to warfare and the disruptions it caused, were a fraction of those in the Borders.

The Borders was a community that had seen the rise and fall of the Reiving society. As the Border families rode stealing and burning as they went, did witches too creep through the night to steal and ultimately burn? This may have had something to do with it but again comparisons throw up more anomalies. The Reivers had ridden their way across the Borders but also into Galloway and down over Northumbria. For every witchcraft trial that took place in Galloway there were around five in the Borders. And the trials in Northumbria were a tenth of what they were on the Scottish side. Warfare and the Reivers played their part in shaping Borders life and attitudes but, like the harsh rural life, cannot be the main factor in the high levels of trials and executions.

While the Borders psyche was, and many would argue still is, distinct in many ways is that enough to explain the high levels of accusations? It may have been Borderers that laid accusations but they were equally those who were accused. The main players in the trials that encouraged those accusations and sat in judgement over the accused were the Kirk Ministers and Elders.

So what of the Kirk in the Borders? Between 1600 and 1700 the Scottish Kirk endured upheaval and change: from the changes of the Reformation, the signing of the covenant, trials with the King and the imposition of bishops, civil war and the commonwealth. At the same time as this turbulence was occurring the Kirk managed to deal with the highest number of witchcraft trials in its history. Internal church upheaval about forms of worship were mirrored in external attacks by the Devil. Religion and the Kirk had changed radically in Scotland since the Reformation. Religious belief, previously an accepted but placid way of life for the majority under the Catholic faith, became an intense personal duty. Individuals were to be constantly on their guard against the Devil. The comforting protection of the local parish priest was gone and a terrifying need for spiritual salvation had arrived in its place. Spiritual laxity could no longer be tolerated. Belief in and defence of the true faith was all consuming. The new faith, strong in its zeal, was nonetheless well aware of the threats surrounding God's elect.

The Kirk in the Borders underwent the same crises as the Kirk elsewhere but its very proximity to the border with England meant an increased exposure to the elements of war and all its uncertainties. Little wonder then that they felt themselves to be particularly under siege by the Devil and his hordes of witches. The belief that the Devil attacked the most Godly took hold in the Borders and under threat the Kirk responded in kind. Perhaps it was that factor that tipped the balance in the Borders.

The Borders was a land of rural communities, worn down by the fragility of poor rural existence and with a recent history of Reivers in the night. They also suffered the ravages of recent and, no doubt to them, seemingly unending warfare. They had had to endure plague and famine. These stresses would have been articulated and thus relieved by accusations of witchcraft. Someone had to be to blame. However, accusations and activities that would have been firmly dealt with in previous times with harsh condemnation, excommunication and some form of punishment, were now ruthlessly pursued to the furthest extent of the law by Kirk Elders in the Borders. Witchcraft was no longer seen as a misguided activity but as a diabolical evil.

Witchcraft was a real and genuine fear in Scotland in the late 16th and early 17th centuries and should not just be dismissed as the foolishness of ill educated common people. Belief in the spirit world and supernatural power in a time before modern medicine and rational belief helped to make sense of an often cruel and harsh existence. What had been around for several hundred years as a relatively harmless belief system with many positive benefits became a victim of a particular set of circumstances. War, famine, plague and religious upheaval all combined to turn belief in the power of witchcraft to a fear of witches. It is difficult for the modern mind to conceive of the ease with which fear of witches could consume a community. What is worth recalling is the role of the Kirk in the Borders in taking that fear and turning it into hysteria. The Kirk perceived themselves to be under attack because of their very Godliness. Their response was to unleash a wave of torture and ill treatment that would consume every village and town in the Borders and cost at least two hundred and eighteen people their lives.

In 1736, the Scottish Witchcraft Act was formally repealed by Parliament. It was replaced by the Witchcraft Act of the British Isles. Ostensibly decriminalising witchcraft it relegated witches to the jurisdiction of the churches. It also demanded a much higher emphasis on real evidence and introduced a more rigorous approach to proofs. Confession, so important previously but so open to abuse under interrogation, would no longer be considered as absolute proof. The modern world was dawning with a greater understanding of and faith in science and hard fact. The age of superstition was slipping away.

While many in the Kirk were aware of the danger of abuses where witchcraft trials were undertaken, their belief in witchcraft remained unshaken. While they might support the introduction of some form of rigour in the case of evidence many privately still held to the belief in confession as proof positive. They, afterall, lived in the real world of towns and villages where crops still failed and babies still died for unknown reasons that the new sciences could still not explain. In 1773, the divines of the Associated Presbytery of Scotland passed a resolution affirming their belief in witchcraft.

In 1830 Sir Walter Scott's Letters on *Demonology and witchcraft* was published. The *Letters* is a wide ranging thesis on supernatural beliefs and tales including much besides witchcraft. Scott was able to draw on many local anecdotes for the book despite its basic premise being that no-one believed in such nonsense any more. The Enlightenment had apparently done its work and superstitious beliefs had been banished to the history books lingering on only in folk memories and a few local customs.

But perhaps there was more than just memory to be discovered. Letter nine contains several stories of witchcraft beliefs and trials but finishes with a curious tale. This anecdote tells of a farmer who met a woman who cursed him with such vehemence he felt it necessary to go the Sheriff. When the Sheriff approached the woman she, far from denying the act, was quite as ease with the powers that she had. All three, the farmer, the woman and the Sheriff found the existence of supernatural powers perfectly normal. The story, which Scott claimed was true, had taken place in the Scottish Borders in 1800.

APPENDIX A

Chronology of Events

- *1484 Pope Inocent VIII published his Papal Bull against witches*
- *1563 Scottish Witchcraft Act Passed*
- *1564 John Knox declares witches to be enemies of God*
- *1590 North Berwick witches attempt to drown King James VI*
- *1597 King James VI writes his great book on withcraft, Daemonologie*
- *1600 Outbreak of plague*
- *1607 Outbreak of plague*
- *1623 Famine*
- *1624 Outbreak of plague*
- *1630 Outbreak of plague*
- *1635 Outbreak of plague and famine*
- *1640 General Assembly passes Condemnatory Act against witches*
- *1643 General Assembly passes Condemnatory Act against witches*
- *1644 General Assembly passes Condemnatory Act against witches*
- *1644 Outbreak of plague and famine*
- *1645 General Assembly passes Condemnatory Act against witches*
- *1648 Famine*
- *1649 General Assembly passes Condemnatory Act against witches*
- *1675 Famine*
- *1695 Famine*
- *1700 Last witch executed in the Borders*
- *1722 Last witch executed in Scotland*
- *1736 Scottish Witchcraft Act was formally repealed by Parliament and replaced with the Witchcraft Act which placed much greater emphasis on real proofs and evidence*
- *1773 Divines of the Associated Presbytery of Scotland passed a resolution affirming their belief in witchcraft*

APPENDIX B

The Border Witches

Between 1590 and 1722 around 3,837 witches trials were carried in Scotland. This number comes from existing records. While these are probably the majority of cases new records continue to be found and although the final figure may never be known it will probably be greater than 4,000.

Fate of the Border Witches

Ex = Executed, Op = Other punishment, A = Acquitted, DD = Diet Deserted, Un = Unknown fate

Ayton - 12 : 7Ex, 1Op, 4Un

Annan - 1: 1Un

Berwickshire - 35: 26Ex, 3Op, 6Un

Chirnside - 4: 20p, 2Un

Cockburnspath - 2: 1Ex, 1Un

Coldingham - 15: 10Ex, 5Un

Coldstream- 11: 8Ex, 3Un

Duns - 14: 8Ex, 1A, 5Un

Earlston - 2: 2Un

Eyemouth - 34: 24Ex, 2A, 20p, 6Un

Fountainhall - 1: 1Un

Galashiels - 9: 5Ex, 4Un

Greenlaw - 2: 2Un

Heriot - 1: 1Un

Innerleithen - 6: 3Ex, 1Op, 2Un

Jedburgh - 35: 23Ex, 3A, 10p, 8Un

Kelso - 16: 12Ex, 3Op, IUn

Lauder - 15: 7Ex, 8Un

Lilliesleaf - 4: 1Ex, 3Un

Melrose - 19: 16Ex, 2Op, 1Un

Moffat - 2: 2Un

Paxton -3: 3Un

Peebles - 61: 41Ex, 1A, 8Op, 11Un

Romano - 1: 1Un

Roxburgh - 9: 3Ex, 4Op, 2Un

Selkirk - 27: 20Ex, 2Op, 5Un

Stobo - 3: 2DD, 1Un

Stow - 7: 6Ex, 1Un

Traquair - 1: 1Un

Total Border total = 352 individuals tried, 218 were executed, 15 died in gaol due to torture and ill treatment, 9 committed suicide. *(These numbers come from existing records. The true number may possibly be higher.)*

APPENDIX C

Scottish witch trials

While the population of early modern Scotland was more evenly distributed than it is today, the Borders was still a relatively sparsely populated area. As such, the number of trials is much higher than would be anticipated. Strathclyde and the West, Central Scotland and Grampian were all more populous that the Borders but had far fewer trials.

The records of witchcraft cases are frustratingly piecemeal in many cases. George Black's *Calendar of Cases of Witchcraft in Scotland 1510 to 1727* in combination with Larner, Hyde Lee and McLachlan's *Source book of Scottish Witchcraft* list many of the known cases. The most comprehensive database of trial records was compiled by the University of Edinburgh between 2001 and 2003 although new records continue to be uncovered.

Database source - Julian Goodare, Lauren Martin, Joyce Miller and Louise Yeoman, 'The Survey of Scottish Witchcraft', http://www.arts.ed.ac.uk/witches/ (archived January 2003, accessed Oct-Dec 2007).

Number of witchcraft trials
922 Edinburgh and the Lothians (shipping area and Capital, contained the High courts and so drew in cases from across the entire country)
352 Borders
342 Strathclyde and the west
323 Fife
297 Central Scotland
257 Grampian including Aberdeen
248 Galloway
204 Highlands and Islands
183 Banff, Angus, Kincardine
 87 Orkney and Shetland
625 unknown areas

BIBLIOGRAPHY

Black, G.F., *Calendar of Cases of Witchcraft in Scotland 1510 to 1727* (Kessinger Publishing 2000)

Brown, N.P., *Pagans and Priests* (Lion Hudson 2006)

Cantor, N.F., *In the Wake of the Plague* (Simon & Shuster UK Ltd 2001)

Cawthorne, N., *Witch Hunt* (Arcturus Publishing Ltd 2002)

Davidson, T., *Rowan tree and red thread* (Oliver and Boyd 1949)

Ewan, E & Meickle, M. (eds.), *Women in Scotland*, c.1100-c.1750 (Tuckwell Press, 1999)

Goodare, J., *The Scottish witch-hunt in context* (Manchester University press 2002)

Institoris, *Malleus maleficarum* (1486)

Jillings, K., *Scotland's Black Death* (Tempus publishing Limited 2003)

Knox, J., *The First Blast of the Trumpet against the Monstrous Regiment of Women* (1558)

Kors, A.C., Peters, E., *Witchcraft in Europe 400 - 1700* (University of Pennsylvania Press 2001)

Lamont-Brown, R., *Scottish Witchcraft* (Chambers 1994)

Larner, C., *Enemies of God* (Chatto & Windus 1981)

Larner, C., Hyde Lee, C., McLachlan, H., *Source book of Scottish Witchcraft* (The Grimsay Press 2005)

Linton, E. L., *Witch Stories* (Chapman and Hall London 1861)

Maidment, J., *Spottiswoode Miscellany* Vol ii (Edinburgh 1845)

Marshall, K., *John Knox* (Birlinn Limited 2000)

Maxwell-Stuart, P.G., *An Abundance of Witches* (Tempus Publishing Limited 2005)

Maxwell-Stuart, P.G., *Satan's Conspiracy* (Tuckwell Press 2001)

Maxwell-Stuart, P.G., *Witchcraft A History* (Tempus Publishing Limited 2000)

Maxwell-Stuart, P.G., *Witch Hunters* (Tempus Publishing Limited 2003)

Moffat, A., *The Reivers* (Birlinn Limited 2007)

Murray, M., *The God of the Witches* (Sampson Low 1941)

Normand, L., Roberts, G., *Witchcraft in Early Modern Scotland* (University of Exeter Press 2000)

Scott, G.R., *A History of Torture* (Senate Publishing 1994)

Scott, W., *Letters on Demonology and Witchcraft* (Wordsworth Editions Limited 2001)

Stuart, J., *Daemonologie* (Edinburgh 1591)

REFERENCES

1) Manuscript Sources
National Archives of Scotland, Edinburgh

2) Database Sources
Julian Goodare, Lauren Martin, Joyce Miller and Louise Yeoman, 'The Survey of Scottish Witchcraft', http://www.arts.ed.ac.uk/witches/ (archived January 2003, accessed Oct-Dec 2007).

Chapter 2
Larner, C., *Enemies of God* (Chatto & Windus 1981)
Register of the Privy Council, Second Series, Vol 3, pp.170; 391

Chapter 3
Brown, N.P., *Pagans and Priests* (Lion Hudson 2006)
Lamont-Brown, R., *Scottish Witchcraft* (Chambers 1994)
Murray, M., *The God of the Witches* (Sampson Low 1941)
Register of the Privy Council, Second Series, Vol 4, pp.15; 55; 80; 98; 131; 316
Register of the Privy Council, Second Series, Vol 3, pp.361; 378; 389
Register of the Privy Council, Second Series, Vol 3, p.443
Register of the Privy Council, Second Series, Vol 3, pp.397-400
Scottish Justiciary Court VI pp.143; 147
Register of Royal Letters, Vol 1, p.377, Vol 2, pp.418; 553

Chapter 4
Maidment, J., *Spottiswoode Miscellany* Vol ii (Edinburgh 1845)
Books of Adjournal JC 2/7 fo 148v 154r
Books of Adjournal JC2/7 fo 160r 168
Fasti 2.36
Register of the Privy Council, Second Series, Vol 5, pp.176-77; 572
Register of the Privy Council, Second Series, Vol 5, pp.593-594
Register of the Privy Council, Second Series, Vol 5, p.605

Chapter 5

Maxwell-Stuart, P.G., *Witch Hunters* (Tempus Publishing Limited 2003)

Register of the Privy Council, Third Series, Vol 1, pp.251-2

Register of the Privy Council, Third Series, Vol 1, p.210

Chapter 6

Maxwell-Stuart, P.G., *An Abundance of Witches* (Tempus Publishing Limited 2005)

Institoris, *Malleus maleficarum* (1486)

Committee of Estates PA11/8fo.172r

Chapter 7

Scott, G.R., *A History of Torture* (Senate Publishing 19940

Register of the Privy Council, Third Series, Vol 1, p.221

Edinburgh Magazine, Vol 1, p.201

Chapter 8

Goodare, Julian., *The Scottish witch-hunt in context* (Manchester University press 2002)

Larner, C., Enemies of God (Chatto & Windus 1981)

Acts of the Parliament of Scotland, Vol 3, p.44

Book of the Universall Kirk, Vol 1, pp.343-4

Chapter 9

Moffat, A., *The Reivers* (Birlinn Limited 2007)

Circuit Court Book JC 10/2 fo. 210r

High Court Process Notes JC2/13f.76v

Process Notes JC26/38

Chapter 10

Larner, C., Enemies of God (Chatto & Windus 1981)

Circuit Court Books JC10/3 fo.26v.,50r

Circuit Court Books JC10/3 fo.26v.,50r

Chapter 11

Larner, C., *Enemies of God* (Chatto & Windus 1981)

Goodare, Julian., *The Scottish witch-hunt in context* (Manchester University press 2002)

INDEX